PARENTING
for the First Time
Getting Off to a Healthy Start

PARENTING
for the First Time
Getting Off to a Healthy Start

Dale R. Olen, Ph.D.

A Life Skills Parenting Book

JODA Communications, Ltd.

Milwaukee, Wisconsin

Editor: Chris Roerden
Design & Layout: Chris Roerden & Associates
Copyright 1994 by Dale R. Olen, Ph.D.
All rights reserved

Published by: JODA Communications, Ltd.
10125 West North Avenue
Milwaukee, WI 53226

PRINTED IN THE UNITED STATES OF AMERICA

Publisher's Cataloging in Publication

Olen, Dale R.
      Parenting for the first time: getting off to a healthy start /
Dale R. Olen.
      p. cm. -- (Life skills parenting series; no. 1)
      Includes index.
      ISBN 1-56583-015-6

      1. Child psychology. 2. Parenting—Psychological aspects.
3. Child development.   I. Title. II. Series.

BF721.044 1994   155.4
                                                QB194-1392

Table of Contents

page

Introduction

Parenting for the First Time

You're soon to give birth to a living human child. She (or is it he?) is going to hit the floor running, pockets full of spunk and spark. Awe fills your heart—what an amazing miracle awaits you. But another feeling bumps awe to the background— panic.

Getting pregnant—in most cases—was the easy part. But now what? You complain: "What do I know about being a parent? Sure, I was a kid once (oh, why can't I still be one?), and I saw how my folks did it. Some of what they did was fine and some wasn't. But that seems so long ago. What do I do now when I bring my daughter or son home from the hospital— and for the next 18 years?"

You're about to become a parent. But parents were the enemy, weren't they? And they were always so "old." Now you're about to become one of them.

Throughout this pregnancy you have already experienced the full range of emotions: one moment you feel giddy, the next overwhelmed, then unsure, ecstatic, subdued, confident, frantic and hopeful. Overall, I hope you are excited by the coming of your child and are anticipating with joy and delight the birth of the child you *want*. But I understand, because of your circumstances, that you may be dreading this birth. Perhaps you are a single, teenaged woman who wanted pregnancy as much as you wanted a tooth pulled without Novocain.

Whatever your feelings, you've made the choice to bring this child to life and to raise her or him to the best of your ability. In awe, then, you come to this incredible moment—your child is about to be born. You've done the breathing exercises. You've watched the movies. You've faithfully performed your stretching and relaxing routines. All is ready for the birth. But now what?

I wish at the moment of your child's birth you would be infused with all the parenting skills you need to raise your son or daughter well. But the skills and attitudes of parenting must be learned through "on-the-job training." You learn with your first child.

You experiment. You read. You talk with friends and family about what to do and not do. Some things work and some fail badly.

When you begin parenting you need a quick checklist of principles to start with. That's what I've given you in this book. It contains the essential ingredients to becoming the best parent you can be. You build your parenting skills on the fundamentals presented here. Throughout your parenting career, whenever you need to return to the basics, just pick up this book and review the principles of how to mother and father your child.

I write this book to you as I approach the end of my formal parenting time. My children are in their late teen years now. I have loved parenting them. There have been many wonderful, life-giving experiences we've shared together, along with some difficult, painful moments as well. My children have taught me a lot about parenting, and I hope I have taught them some things about living full and satisfying lives.

I know how difficult parenting is, but I also know how satisfying and fulfilling it can be as well. I believe you will have a rich and marvelous experience of parenting your children if you understand and follow the basic principles I will share with you in this book.

You need specific skills to parent well. Those

you can learn. Add to those skills a deep and uncon-
ditional love for your children, and your journey for
the next 25 years will produce children that bring a
smile to your face and warmth to your heart.

Chapter 1

Can You Really Get Ready?

When my wife and I married I was finishing up my training as a psychologist. She was teaching middle school. We both worked with children. I had formally studied them—how they develop, what to expect at different ages, how to work with them as they grow up.

When we found out that Joelyn was pregnant, we began to read—with the appetite of a dog on steroids (they don't stop eating!)—about raising a child. We read every book we could find on parenting, hoping to prepare ourselves perfectly for our son's entrance into the world.

The day came—September 14, 1975. Joelyn went into labor and I talked with her about breathing! She worked hard and delivered our son, Andy, and I was still talking about breathing. We were thrilled. Two days later, I had the house all ready. I went to pick up Joelyn and Andy and bring them home. I had a meal cooking on the stove. We were parents and we were going to do this job right. We knew what we were doing.

Andy slept in the car. What a perfect child! We got home and laid him in his new crib in his new room. We held each other and watched him sleep peacefully. We tiptoed out of the bedroom. I invited Joelyn to sit on the couch. I poured a glass of wine for both of us and toasted our new life as a family.

As we took our first quiet sip, Andy started to whimper ever so slightly. We panicked. We jumped up and rushed to the bedroom, quickly picking him up. Now he was crying full force. How do you stop this, we wondered. Joelyn fed him. He continued crying. Next she held him closely, talking to him softly. That didn't work. I held him and talked to him softly. No change. We figured his diaper was wet. Joelyn checked. It was stone dry. But she changed his diaper anyway. We didn't know.

Then we discovered the cure—holding him in the crook of our arm, half-way over our shoulder and walking him somewhat quickly around the room. First Joelyn did it for ten minutes. She was getting exhausted. Remember she had just delivered this little guy two days earlier. So I took over and walked him for ten minutes. Then I got tired. Remember I was the one who had been talking to Joelyn about breathing all the time she was in labor. Our wine sat on the coffee table aging to a finer vintage.

After 45 minutes, Andy was sleeping in my arms. I laid him gently in his crib. Ah, it worked. We sat down to eat the wonderful meal I had prepared. Just as Joelyn sat down, Andy woke up again! Once more, we flew to his room, picked him up and spent another 45 minutes comforting him and wondering what we were doing wrong. Finally he fell sound asleep and we sat down to our meal. I presented it— burned to a crisp, dry, tasteless and totally unappetizing. We sat across from each other, looked at our food, raised our eyes, found one another, and both of us spontaneously burst into tears. We went to the couch, sat in each other's arms and cried.

But we were so happy! Why these tears? At that moment, we realized a couple of things. One was our quiet, intimate fun-filled life together—just the two of us—was over for at least the next 25 years or so. We felt sad. So this was "post-partum depression!" I had read about it, but never thought we'd feel it. We *wanted* children. We were excited and happy about Andy's birth. We couldn't wait to become parents.

But no matter how wonderful it all was to parent a child, we realized we were losing something too— we were losing our way of being close to each other without any intruders. That was the word—intruder. Andy was an *intruder.* We almost choked when the word came out of our mouths. But that's what he was. He had invaded our lives. He wouldn't let us sit quietly on the couch and have a glass of wine. He interfered with my plans for a good meal with Joelyn. He kept us awake at night. He forced us to stay home on weekends.

So this was what having a child was all about. Well, no, just partially. We quickly got over our tears. We soon realized that we didn't need to pick up our child every time he stirred in his crib. Quickly we learned to love him and found ourselves enjoying almost every sound and movement he made. Although we thought we had prepared ourselves to be parents, we realized that reading the books and watching our parents when we were kids wasn't enough training for the task ahead of us. By and large, we would become parents through trial-and-error and by using our best instincts of love and commitment to our son.

Your experiences as a parent will be unique. When your first child comes home from the hospital, you may not cry as we did. Your welcome-home meal might turn out just fine, even though ours didn't. No one can predict and prepare you fully for what you will experience. You and your baby will develop unique ways of behaving and relating to each other. The complete master plan for how to parent in every situation cannot be given to you.

But in the calm, before the birth, you can think about being a parent and how you will want to be for your child. You can sit back and realize you are entering a time of fullness. You will work harder than you ever have before. You will know more joy and delight than you thought possible. You will worry and feel fear like never before. You will read books to your child about green eggs and ham that make no sense to you, and you will talk again like the baby you once were yourself. You will regain the child in you as you see the world through your child's eyes. But you will also take on the role of parent—a role that will sometimes feel uncomfortable and other times will feel so natural to you that it will make you wonder if you weren't born to parent.

As you reflect on how you want to parent, let me offer you a reality check so you understand what you're getting into. I've been through this parenting business, and I've worked with hundreds—even thousands—of people who have laughed and cried their way from births to graduations. I want you to know what you can expect on becoming a parent.

If you know what to expect, you can react more gracefully when those things happen. If your expectations are too high, you will become disappointed, frustrated and perhaps angry when you or your kids don't measure up. On the other hand, if your expectations are too low, you and your children may never achieve the heights of excitement and growth possible in family life. I'd like you to be realistic about parenting—to anticipate the joys and delights that sparkle throughout these family years—and to understand the stresses and strains that occur every day with kids growing up.

Do you want the good news or the bad news first? Since most people seem to want the bad news first, let's start there.

Bad News

1. You feel less free.

Right from the beginning, you notice you stay home more than before. During those first couple of months, cocooning at home feels just fine. You want to stay close to your baby. If you're the mother, you might not even care to go out because you're still recuperating from the labor and delivery. You just like sitting quietly, while Dad changes diapers and crib sheets.

After a while, however, you want—and need—to get out. But whom do you leave your daughter with? Some kid baby-sitter? A neighbor you hardly know? Who can be trusted? Who can fulfill the awesome responsibility of caring for this most precious child? Of course, your parents come to mind. But they're in Florida for the winter. You're not even sure about your younger sister, who is a nice kid. But she probably wants that creepy boyfriend of hers to come along. You don't want your baby around him, that's for sure. So you stay home until late Spring when your folks return and give you the break, by now, that you desperately need.

You won't like that your personal freedom is restricted. You long for the opportunity again to come and go as you please. You feel the burden of responsibility. Once your baby comes, you not only have to take care of yourself, but now you have to do everything for this very dependent little creature who needs you to stay alive. She lies there totally helpless, looking to you for food, comfort and safety. That burden can weigh you down and constrain the carefree who-gives-a-darn attitude you knew B.C. (before children).

When your children get to school age, they become more involved in after-school activities that demand your time and presence. They dance, sing, practice soccer, tennis and basketball. On the weekends, you find yourself scheduling around their activities. By the time they reach late preteen and teen years, they begin going out on weekend evenings. That, of course, means you must drive them to and fro, and remain home in case they call. Personal freedom feels like a friend you knew in another life.

2. You, especially the mother, experience fatigue.

Many times, young mothers, anxious to get on with mothering, come home from the hospital and jump right into the parenting tasks. After a very short time, they hit the wall of fatigue.

I want you to realize how significant was the trauma that occurred to your body. You put in a lot of work these past nine months, feeding that life inside you and hauling around this little giant. Then came the labor and delivery. As a man, I cannot fully appreciate the impact and the drain on your body of carrying a baby, but it's got to be great. After the delivery, your body doesn't want to do much. It's very tired and needs to rest. But your baby doesn't know that. So when he's hungry, no matter what the hour, he lets you know. And you'd better respond. That works great for your baby, but your body is crying out for rest and quiet.

Please try to take it easy. Don't attempt to become "Super Mom" in the first month or so. You can always do that later. Although you probably want to be involved with your child's every tiny movement, try to let go a little and rest. Let Dad pick him up and change him and wash him and rock him too.

Expect to feel tired at the beginning until your body recovers. After that, continue expecting to feel tired, because you will be putting in long hours with your first, your second, and maybe your third or fourth child. The more children you have the more tired you will feel.

3. Your children become your consuming priority.

Children are the "squeaky wheels" that get the grease. Because they are so dependent, they demand your time and attention. They become your top priority. No matter what your priority list looked like before children, once they arrive, they shoot right to the top. Before children, most adults claim their careers or a significant adult relationship as their top priority. Theoretically, once they become parents, they may still say their marriage or the job is top priority. But for most people, the children, in fact, take over that number one spot.

You need to work on balancing your priorities. In particular, you need to attend to your marriage, keeping it up there near the top. I like to think parents can have a double top priority: the marriage and the children. One of your best gifts to your children is a cooperative, loving marriage.

If your career has always been a priority, it will probably remain so. It's easier to keep your work a priority because you usually leave home for a set number of hours a day. You are away from the children and can give yourself over to your work fully. The danger, of course, is that your work may become such a high priority that the children and your marriage suffer. Again, balancing your priorities becomes the important skill. More on that later.

In healthy, happy families I always see parents setting up their priorities in the following way:

Priorities of Successful Parents
1. Marriage and children
2. Career
3. Upkeep of home
4. Other personal relationships
5. Personal hobbies and recreation

For many people, their personal religious faith flows throughout these priorities, and that's why I didn't list it as a separate dimension.

4. Parenting becomes more difficult as your children grow up.

I know it seems as if it should get easier as the kids grow up, but I want you to know from the start that it doesn't. In fact, it seems to get more difficult, even though you gain more freedom. When your children are little, the demands are mostly physical. You have to do everything for them. About the only psychological demand occurs when they get sick, and you worry about them. You feel so bad for them because they have such little tolerance for pain and discomfort.

As your children grow up, they become more complex. They gradually "lose their innocence."

They begin to say "no." They no longer obey just because you say so. Pretty soon, they begin asking "Why?" to your every command. They learn to deceive you, to remain silent and to sulk. They reveal moods and feelings you never saw in them before.

As they go through their teen years, you feel as though you are losing control and influence in their lives. In fact, you are. Your worry and concern grow by leaps and bounds. Whereas you used to be physically exhausted from caring for your toddler, you are now emotionally exhausted from dealing with your teenager. The strain on you psychologically is greater when you discover that your teenager has been smoking in his bedroom than when he got upset as a six-year-old because he couldn't hit a baseball very well.

For now, you need pay attention only to your soon-to-be-born child. But tuck away, somewhere in the back of your mind, that you don't reach the top of the parenting mountain once Sarah can go to the toilet by herself. You'll have to work hard on parenting, probably until the children leave home— and then some.

Good News

1. Your personal freedom returns in stages.

The bad news I mentioned earlier was that you lose personal freedom when you become a parent.

The good news is you can gradually reclaim it. At specific times during your child's development you will experience again the sense of liberation and freedom you once knew. When you regain your freedom you will appreciate it so much more than before children.

What am I talking about? There are certain events in the life of your child that you will enjoy more than your child will. These moments are watershed experiences that allow you to break into a renewed sense of personal freedom. Each time one of these events takes place, you will jump up, raise both your arms in the air, and cry out, "Free at last! Thank God Almighty, I'm free at last." What are those events?

Events that free parents

1. Child is finally toilet-trained!
2. Child can dress herself.
3. Child goes to school all day.
4. Child no longer needs formal child-care programs.
5. Child no longer needs a baby-sitter.
6. Child can drive the car (even though worries may surround this activity).
7. Child leaves home for school or work (sadness accompanies the sense of freedom).
8. Child is totally self-sufficient, especially financially.

When each of these events takes place, you and your parenting partner deserve to go out and celebrate. Really, these are great moments, not only because they free you from a parenting task, but because your child—with your help—has navigated another stage of growing up. Think of it. What an accomplishment for a child to urinate in a toilet instead of in his or her diapers. And ultimately, what a maturing act for this child to leave home, a self-sufficient, independent young adult, able to journey through the world on his or her own. You will have been a part of that development. So celebrate. When the time comes, pat yourself on the back for a job well done by you and your child. And raise your hand to the sky, thumb-up, and shout, "Yes, she can dress herself."

2. You'll never know love like you have for your child.

In no other relationship do you experience love like you do with your child. It stands out as the purest form of loving that is capable to human beings. While other loving relationships involve a loop (your love goes out to someone, but some form of love almost always returns to you), your love as a parent shoots like an arrow directly to your child. You can love your child without any return.

Over the years, I've come to realize that parental love is the only altruistic love around. It gives without seeking a return. Oh, don't get me wrong. A return is nice. You love it when your children love you back—and they do. But you don't make their "return love" a condition for your loving them. They're your kids, and you love them no matter what.

There may be times you don't *like* your children very much. But you always love them.

Your love for your children demands a heroism you don't know you have. You do difficult things for them without counting the cost. When my daughter Amy was one year old, she awoke one night (these things always happen at night) with a very high temperature. The only way we knew to reduce her fever was to place her in a cool tub of water. But she would have none of that.

As soon as we attempted to put her in the tub she began wailing and resisting. I knew she liked playing with water toys, so I decided *I* would have to get in the bathtub *with* her and her toys.

So at two o'clock in the morning, I'm climbing into a tub of cool water so my daughter's temperature will go down. To this day, I remind her of the depth of my love for her based on my "heroic" deed years ago.

You give to your children 24 hours a day. You are available to them when they need you. You keep them in your own personal center, feeling with them, concerned for them, remembering their activities. Whereas in all other relationships you eventually return to your own center, with your children you stay focused on them and their needs. Although such love fatigues you at times, it also feels tremendously fulfilling and satisfying.

To love another person just for his or her own sake captures the very core of being a human being. When you love your children deeply—and you will—you become what you were made to be, a full and giving person.

3. You get to be a kid again.

What fun! You play "house," but this time for real. You enjoy the activity of caring for a helpless baby, rocking her in your lap, taking her for walks, dressing her up and showing her off to the grandparents. You read nursery rhymes again, play little board games and enjoy all the new dolls available. You watch "Sesame Street" and "Mr. Rogers" with your child, and get into those programs as much as your child does.

You get to teach your child new skills, such as baseball, bike riding, making snow figures and roller-skating. And while you teach, you get to do those things again yourself. You have the chance once more to get silly and giddy. You can goof around without it having to make sense. You are free again to be a child and enjoy the moment.

4. You get to see the world through your child's eyes.

You develop a new view of the world once you have children. They surprise you with their perception of everything from Grandpa's big nose to how television pictures come into your house. You delight in their creative imagination. You meet their imaginary friends and pets that, by the way, never shed. You marvel at their illogical logic and their intuitive jumps to profound truths. Most importantly, you have the chance to feel the awe they experience when they see a waterfall for the first time, watch a Christmas tree being decorated or find an Easter basket left by the bunny. All these insights and discoveries you will enjoy right along with your child.

5. You gain great satisfaction from watching your child grow up.

Although there are bumps along the way, you know the excitement of your child learning skills for living a full life. Right from the beginning, you will be thrilled with your child's ability to raise himself up from his stomach, then give you a smile of recognition afterwards. You'll be ecstatic when he creeps, then stands, then walks, then talks. Imagine what joy you'll know when your daughter can count to ten, say the alphabet and point to all the parts of her body.

As your child grows up, she learns to ride a two-wheeled bike, cross the street by herself and answer the phone. (Later on in teen years, you may wish this was one skill she wouldn't have learned so well.) She learns to make and keep friends, fight with her brother, stand up for herself, shoot three-point baskets, do ballet, write essays, compute math and drive a car.

You will be excited for your child growing up. You will be proud of her accomplishments. Although you'll worry too, you will find that your child is growing up to be a great and wonderful young adult. How satisfying that will be for you. The sense of well-being that you experience will be a wonderful reward for your loving care of this young human being. It makes parenting well worth the while.

Chapter 2

Your Changing Roles as a Parent

You don't just become a parent and that's it. You grow into parenting when your first child is born. And you grow out of it as your child passes through the teen years. In other words, as a parent you change, and you need to change as your child grows up. You cannot parent a newborn infant as you do a toddler. You cannot parent a toddler as you do a preteen. And definitely you cannot parent teenagers as you parent any other age group of children.

As your children grow up and change, you also need to grow, adapt, change, modify, improvise and adjust your style as a parent. Depending on the age of your child, you sometimes play the role of nurturer, sometimes authority, often consultant and finally a friend. At times you play all those roles simultaneously.

In many parenting courses, you are told how your children develop. Instructors and authors explain the various stages of growth in children. By ten months your child will begin walking. By one and a half years he will be talking. By two and a half he will be toilet trained. By 10 he will be bouncing back and forth between independence from you and a continued strong dependence on you. As a teenager you can expect him to be breaking away from home in a strong and significant way. Of course, a lot of smaller twists and turns take place in between these significant stages. But you get the idea.

Your child evolves and grows. But so do you as the parent. Just as your child goes through fairly well-defined stages of development, you as a parent also need to evolve through stages. In broad strokes, here are the stages you must go through that correspond to the stages of your child:

Stages of Parental Growth		
STAGE	CHILD	PARENT
1	Totally dependent (0–7 months)	Nurturer
2	Exploring and testing limits (7 months–10 years)	Authority
3	Striving for independence (10–19 years)	Consultant
4	Becoming interdependent (over 20; they lead their own lives, but need you as a friend)	Friend

As the parent you need to evolve through four specific stages of growth. If you grow as your child grows, your relationship and effectiveness with your child will be strong and helpful. But if you get stuck in one of the stages along the way and your child keeps on growing, you will run into major conflicts with your child.

The main sticking point in your development as a parent will come between the stages of Authority and Consultant. This transition is not a natural one. It has to be worked on. If you don't gradually move to stage three (Consultant) as your daughter moves to stage three (Striving for Independence), you will run into a buzz saw of stress, the likes of which you can now only imagine. As your child grows, so must you. Here, then, are the stages of parenting that you must enter:

Nurturer

This first stage comes naturally to most parents. I'm sure you will get right into it. When that helpless little creature becomes part of your family, you spontaneously and easily love him and respond to his every need. In his state of sheer dependency, this eight pounds of human life elicits from you that warm and tender dimension known as motherly or fatherly love. You jump to feed, cloth, cuddle, bounce baby on your knee, carry him everywhere and change his diapers. (You may not jump as quickly on that one. In fact, you might find yourself waiting to see if your parenting partner makes the first move.)

Nurturing rises up in you naturally. You don't have to work at it. As long as your child is totally dependent, you will function solely as nurturer.

Authority

But very shortly into your baby's life he begins asserting himself. Around seven months of age Tommy begins to creep. Thus begins stage two of development for the child—Testing the Limits. As soon as Tommy starts moving around the house on his own power, you naturally begin the second stage of parenting—Authority. Parental authority arises out of the nurturing role as a form of protecting the child from harm. Through your authority you attempt to keep Tommy safe by setting the limits in which he can navigate.

As soon as Tommy begins to explore, you start using your authority. You set up gates at the stairs; you say "no" when he pokes the dog; you take away the plastic bag he's playing with; you slap his fingers when he tries sticking them into the electrical outlet. All these authoritative moves are solely for Tommy's welfare.

As Tommy gets older you continue using authority for his safety. You insist: "You cannot cross the busy street"; "You must get to bed by seven"; "You must eat all your food."

At this point, the waters of authority can become slightly muddy. You can also begin using authority for reasons other than your child's safety. You can use authoritative power for your own gratification and the satisfaction of your own needs. If Tommy starts yelling at the dog while you're talking on the phone, you may use your authority to quiet him down. It's not for his safety, but rather for your sanity. The same occurs when you insist that your 11-year-old turn down the radio. You do that for your own sake, not for her safety.

These two motives for the use of authority— your child's safety and the gratification of your own needs—get mixed together in daily family life. The effect on children of this mix is confusion. Children find it difficult to interpret parental authority as an act of concern. They often view it as aggression or as the parents' selfish needs to have things their own way.

The reason children have such difficulty with parental authority is that they don't see it as an act of loving concern on your part. They don't see it, because you have used authority to gain your own satisfaction as well as the children's well-being. Authority with children is best used when your concern is the safety and well-being of the children.

You need to set limits to protect your children. But authority that is used to take care of yourself, on the other hand, needs careful discernment. I encourage you to recognize the difference between these two uses of authority, and to use authority to gain your own needs only if all other avenues have been closed.

If you attempt to gain your children's cooperation regarding a need you have and they refuse to respond to your need, then you can use authority. But can you use that authority to help the children learn how to cooperate rather than as a tool for the satisfaction of your needs? In other words, can you use it for *their* sake, *their* growth, rather than as a way of getting what *you* want?

To be used in a human, growing way, authority must be seen as a tool to help the child protect himself or herself physically and psychologically. Its purpose is to aid the child in developing a way of thinking and acting that helps him or her grow personally and interpersonally. Certainly as a parent you have the role of creating rules based on acceptable norms of living. But those rules should always consider, first of all, the child's development as a person, not your gratification as a parent.

For instance, if Laura is making a lot of noise while you talk on the phone, authority can be employed to help her learn appropriate cooperative behavior. This can be accomplished by setting the limits of what Laura can and cannot do when someone is talking on the phone. If she stays within those limits she will experience the social rewards of life in this family. If she steps beyond those limits she will experience the consequences of inappropriate behavior—in this case, perhaps sitting in a corner chair until you are finished with the phone conversation. Thus, Laura learns how to become responsible for her behavior. (You can read much more about teaching your child how to become responsible through discipline by reading the second book of this Life Skills Parenting Series, *The Thoughtful Art of Discipline.*)

Children's major difficulty with parental authority develops because they often interpret all forms of authoritative action as oppressive rather than loving. If you use authority to gratify your own needs, or if you use authority in a strong-armed, verbally or physically violent manner, your children will misinterpret your loving concern for them.

This misunderstanding pains me when I see it in families. The parents love their children; the children love their parents. But the manner in which the parents use authority often drives deeper wedges between themselves and their children. So watch carefully how you use authority. You need to use it, and at times you need to be strong in how you use it.

But always try to use your authority for the physical or psychological safety of the children. If you can keep your own needs free from your use of authority, you will be much more successful in getting your kids to respond to you in a cooperative way.

Consultant

When children begin to think and act independently, you are called to the next role of parenting. You must now begin functioning as a consultant. Two-year-olds begin acting independently. But you need not become a consultant just yet. These toddlers are simply pushing their limits—and yours—to see what the boundaries are. As your children get to be 10 and 11 years of age, they begin thinking more independently and acting that way more consistently.

It's at this time that you need to make the major shift from simple *authority* to gradually becoming a *consultant* to your children. This transition stands as one of the most difficult tasks you have as a parent. While the movement from nurturer to authority may have seemed natural and instinctive, the move from authority to consultant feels unnatural and labored. It doesn't just happen by itself. In fact, many parents never take that step from authority to consultant. They remain stuck in their authority role (stage two), while their children are growing into their independent role (stage three). If you don't grow with your children, you will experience much more conflict and stress than if your stages of growth match theirs.

You need to work hard on this transition between authority and consultant. By the time your children are teenagers you must parent them in a style much different from what you used with your toddlers. (As your children grow toward stage three, Striving for Independence, you will definitely want to read *How to Parent Your Teenager* in this Life Skills Parenting Series.)

What does it mean to act as a consultant to your children? To answer that question I want to tell you what a professional consultant does. He or she serves three functions.

Functions of a Consultant

1. Gathers as much information from the client as possible. (For you as a parent this means primarily listening well to your client—your child).
2. Gives information (not mere opinion) about the situation.
3. Based on that information, makes recommendations about what to do.

Your 13-year-old (that must seem far away right now) begins whining about her friend Sarah. She thinks Sarah doesn't like her anymore. She feels sad. You, the loving authoritative parent, jump right in there and save your daughter from her sad feelings. You tell her how silly her thinking is and that Sarah must still like her and she shouldn't worry about it.

Quite honestly, that approach doesn't help a 13-year-old. It might have worked when your daughter was five, but no more. If you want to act as a consultant with your daughter, you respond quite differently. You slow down your own need to save her from her uncomfortable feelings and just listen to her. You ask her questions that allow her to express more of what she feels and believes. Then, after she pours her heart out to you—and feels understood— you can ask her if she'd like to know what you think about her relationship with Sarah.

At that point you take step two in acting as a consultant—you give her information if you have it. So you tell her that Sarah sounded very friendly in the car yesterday when you drove the kids to the mall. You know she called this morning to talk with your daughter. These are signs people use to realize that someone likes them.

Finally, you take step three in consulting. You make a recommendation. You say: "I have a suggestion that might help. Why don't you call Sarah and treat her in a friendly way. Go toward her instead of away from her when you have a doubt about her. I bet you'll find she comes toward you as well." And then you let the discussion go.

As you can see, consultants operate quite differently from authorities. When you parent as an authority you move quickly to save your child from harm. As a consultant you move slowly. As an authority you send messages, telling your child what to do and what not to do. As a consultant you receive messages, listening and keeping quiet. As an authority you issue commands. As a consultant you make recommendations. As an authority you take charge. As a consultant you let go.

Why am I telling you all this now? Your first child may not even be born yet. You don't have to worry about becoming a consultant for years. I tell it to you now because right from the beginning of your relationship with your infant child you need to begin moving toward acting as a consultant. If you wait until your child turns 12, you'll be too late.

Very gradually, you can already begin the process of slowing down your responses, listening well, sharing information and making suggestions. Of course, you'll have to act quickly many times, send commands and insist on certain actions along the way as well. But you need to start early developing your consulting skills, so that when you really need them in those critical teen years, you'll already be a veteran consultant.

Friend

Throughout your relationship to your children you can have moments of friendship. But friendship is based on mutuality and equality. And parents and children don't have that until late in their relationship. You become primarily "friend" when your children leave home and are living independently.

When the children are toddlers and youngsters they are your "buddies" and "pals." But you're still the authority. That's the dominant role. In their teen years you are mainly a consultant. When they move out of the home, finish college, get their first "real" job and sustain themselves financially, then you can become true friends.

Friendship will happen between you and your children if you have navigated the first three stages of parenting well. If you have been a nurturing authority during those early years, and a wise consultant during preteen and teen years, I guarantee you have an excellent chance of a lifelong friendship with your children when they are adults. And that is the greatest reward possible for you, who will have given so much to your children over the years.

Now that you know what the parenting roles are and what you're aiming for, I want to share with you specific principles and tools you need right from the beginning of this wonderful but difficult process of parenting a child.

Chapter 3

Principles and Tools for Parenting Your Children

As soon as your baby is born, you need to begin using the following tools. Sure, right now your baby won't talk back to you if you say it's bedtime. He won't need to be disciplined just yet. Not for several years will he leave his room messy or his towels on the bathroom floor. But you must still begin responding to him with the skills you read about here.

Right from the beginning, it's good to develop a style of parenting, setting up patterns of relating to your child, that will work throughout his early life. Work on these skills from the beginning so *you* get used to them. By the time you really need many of these skills, they will be natural habits you formed from the beginning of your parenting.

A number of the principles and tools here also have to do with your taking care of yourself. Parenting can become an all-absorbing task. As parents you naturally give to your child until you fall exhausted on your bed at the end of the day. I may be exaggerating a bit, but your nurturing love for your child calls forth tremendous psychic energy focused on your child. You will tend not to focus on your own needs.

It is absolutely critical that throughout your parenting career, you take good care of yourself and your other significant relationships, especially your marriage. I'll talk with you later about some things you can do to make sure you remain balanced in your approach to parenting.

Principle 1

**Communicate verbally with your child
from day one and every day.**

Little Patrick was brought home from the hospital by his two proud parents. Shortly afterward, Grandma and Grandpa came over to see their first grandchild. Grandma couldn't wait to hold the tiny bundle and tell him how beautiful he was. After she cooed and gushed for a long time, she asked Grandpa if he'd like to hold the baby. He said: "No, that's all right. I'll wait till he's two years old when he can talk. Then I'll relate to him."

As shocking as that statement might sound, many parents, especially men, believe it. They believe the child can't communicate yet, so there's no point in them communicating with the child. Sounds sort of logical, doesn't it?

In fact, baby Patrick *is* communicating. He may not be saying words, but he's expressing himself as best as he can through sounds and through his body. And more importantly, he's *receiving* messages. Everything you say enters his psychological map and registers in some way. Certainly, he doesn't know the meaning of your words, but he picks up the sense of your emotions. He knows if you like him or not; he senses your warmth toward him; he feels your gentle presence. On the other hand, if you don't make regular contact with him, he experiences your loss; he senses the void that slowly develops in his heart; and he grows like a small plant without water.

How should you communicate regularly with your child? Well, there are a couple of things I'd like to encourage you to do.

1. Realize what it means to communicate.

To communicate means to create a rhythm of *giving and receiving*. To make communication work, you need to receive when your child gives and you need to give when your child can receive. You can't both give at the same time or receive at the same time. Keep this little model in your mind, even though in the first months of life, you will communicate very spontaneously and almost always create the giver-receiver rhythm you need. But by trying to be conscious of this communicating rhythm early on, you start to drill it into your mind and have it in place when your child does become verbal.

2. Make verbal communication with your child as positive as possible.

Again, at the very beginning this occurs easily. You can't imagine ever saying anything negative to your child. She's so adorable. Good. Make as many positive, warm and loving statements as you can. You can't overdo it. Be sure to say them out loud. Don't just think them. And if you're someone who never complimented people much or never expressed love verbally, force yourself to learn now. It's absolutely essential that your child hear from you how wonderful she is—regularly and frequently.

Here's a little suggestion. Whenever you put your child to bed, say something like this to him or her: "Jason, I love you. You are a special person. You are a very good boy who is loving and free and who wants to be the best person he can be." (While your child is still young, read my book *Teaching Children to Like Themselves*. That's where I develop this notion much more.) Right from the beginning, you are sending him or her positive messages that the child takes in at some level and you take in at a very conscious level. Reinforcing your own belief in your child's goodness helps you remain positive with him or her even when things get sticky as the child grows up.

3. Be self-revealing with your children.

The majority of parents send commands and demands, telling their children to pick up the toys or stay out of the street. But they don't share with the children their own feelings and thoughts about themselves or things around them.

If you want your children to relate to you in an

open and expressive way, then your best chance of that happening occurs if you have modeled such open and honest behavior yourself. If you want more than a one-word response from your children as they get older ("fine," "okay," "yeah," "I guess," "I don't know"), then you need to be sharing your own thoughts and feelings with them right from the beginning. By revealing yourself to them, they learn that this is the way they can communicate with others.

So tell your children how you feel about them—that you love them, you like them, you enjoy playing with them. You begin telling them about your feelings even before they can understand. For example, you tell them what happens to you when they cry—"I worry when you cry like that because I don't know what you want. I hope I'm figuring out what you need right now. Let's see if this bottle does the trick." Again, I realize your infant child can't understand your words, but you're teaching her and yourself how to communicate in a family. You are sharing your thoughts and feelings about yourself.

Communicating with your child right from the beginning may be the most important thing you can do for him or her. Keep thinking about the rhythm of communication—giving and receiving. If your child is giving a message, you need to receive it. If you think your child can hear a message, then you can give one. You can't do both at the same time.

Make sure "giving" messages to your child are positive, affirming and frequent. And get into the habit of being self-revealing; that is, talking with your child about how *you* think and feel about things. By doing so you teach your child that the way human beings best connect to each other is through sharing who you are.

Principle 2

Avoid giving your child the silent treatment.

Many times over the past 20 years I have heard adults tell how their parents treated them as children. One of the more unbelievable stories I hear involves a parent who refuses to talk with a child for days or weeks at a time.

Recently, John narrated his experience:

"When I was just a little kid—maybe two or three—I remember Mom getting mad at me for something and then not talking to me. I'd cry and beg her to talk to me and give me a hug, and she'd refuse. I remember at night putting myself to bed, then climbing out of bed, going into Mom's room and asking her to say good night to me. She'd turn her back to me and pretend to sleep. I'd crawl up into her bed and snuggle next to her, hoping she'd turn toward me and talk. She wouldn't do it. I'd go back to my bed believing I was the worst kid in the world."

If you learned that the way to deal with conflict was to turn away from it and pout, then as a parent you need to unlearn that behavior fast. You need to commit yourself to always turning *toward* your child and never *away from* your child. If your daughter offends you, breaks your rules or opposes you, it's never helpful to her or you to turn your back on her and punish her by your silence. Silence hurts relationships. Going toward her and talking with her has a much better chance of improving the relationship.

When children are very small, it won't be too hard to go toward them rather than away from them when they cross you. Let's say your two-year-old yells at you, "Mommy, I hate you." It's the first time he's ever said anything like that to you. You're shocked and hurt. When you get hurt you normally go away and feel bad. You also get angry with the one who hurt you. You show your anger by not talking to that person. Your baby son has just hurt your feelings.

You feel bad, but don't get too angry with him, because he's only two years old. So you don't stop talking to him, even though that's your usual response to hurt. You think: "He's only two. He doesn't really mean it. I know he's just upset." And you turn toward him and tell him, "Danny, I know you're upset with me because I want you to take a nap, but I want you to know it makes me feel bad when you say 'I hate you.' I love you and know you really love me too."

Easy enough. As your child gets older it gets more difficult to go toward him when he opposes you. By the time he hits the teen years, you will return to your old way of dealing with conflict—backing away and giving the silent treatment. You'll think: "He can come to me and apologize. I'll be darned if I'm going to go to him."

Here's precisely where it's important to go toward your son rather than away from him. It's hard—after a disagreement—to knock on his bedroom door before you go to bed and ask him if the two of you are okay with each other. Especially if you feel pushed away by him, it takes heroic effort to go toward him and let him know you still care and you want to resolve the problem between the two of you.

I'm talking with you about something that happens regularly in the teen years—even though you may not have had your first child yet—because you need to develop this "going toward" behavior as soon as your first child is born. Right from the beginning talk with your child. Determine never to deal with your child by turning your back or giving the silent treatment. Decide to take the lead in resolving differences that arise between you and your child.

I have a very strong belief about this issue: It is always up to the parent to move toward the child. The parent should never wait for the child to come to him or her first.

By going toward your child you teach him or her how to handle conflict. You also tell your child that he or she is important enough to you to face whatever the problem is. It tells the child that you value the relationship and that you will do whatever it takes to make sure the relationship remains strong.

Principle 3

Realize that the relationship between you and your child is more important than any issue that separates you.

Again, I tell you this as you begin your parenting journey even though it won't become an issue for a few years. Right now, it seems obvious that the relationship between you and your daughter (or will it be your son?) will always take top priority. But as you move from year to year with your child, conflicts arise that can damage the relationship. By the time your child reaches preteen years, the conflicts can be significant and powerful. You and your child will tend to lock into your positions. You will attempt to persuade each other about how right you are, and in the process you may begin to destroy the relationship between you.

Be very sure about where you want to take a stand. I notice that many parents make federal cases out of little things. Eating supper with a baseball cap on or without elbows on the table can become a battleground issue. Picking up toys can cause major arguments. Being on time can bring parents' feelings to a boiling point. Are these the kind of issues you want to take a stand on? Are you willing to hurt or destroy your relationship with your daughter over these issues? I hope you answer "no."

As you start your parenting life I want you to keep in mind that no issue is big enough for you to be willing to destroy your parent-child relationship. From day one, focus on your relationship with your child. The best formation you can give her, the best foundation you can lay for her is to love her and maintain a close and positive relationship with her. You won't always agree with her nor she with you. But you can still respect and care for each other.

If you develop this attitude and style right from the beginning, it will bear wonderful fruit by the time your kids become teenagers. Nothing is more satisfying to parents than to have a close, caring relationship with their teenaged children. Teenagers can be delightful, interesting and caring. You will be able to enjoy those characteristics in your teenagers if, from the start, you focus on building and maintaining a strong, positive relationship. Keep the issues you disagree on separate from the energy of the relationship.

Principle 4

**Be physical (gently, of course) with
your children.**

Children all the way up to age 15 learn best
through their bodies and through experience, not
through words. Certainly your infant child doesn't
even understand your words. But he does understand your touch. He experiences your presence,
your care and your love when you hold him, kiss
him, pat his head, rub his arm and tussle his hair (if
there is any to tussle). Body to body is the way you
make contact with newborn babies.

What many parents don't realize, though, is that
body contact continues to be important all through
the development of the child. Just last night my 17-
year-old daughter, six inches taller than her mother,
plopped into her mother's lap after supper to snuggle.
That doesn't happen too often anymore, but it re-
minded me that kids still need physical contact no
matter how old they are.

So start out with all the physical touching you
can do, and don't stop when they get older. They

might withdraw at various periods of their development, but they still need a touch, pat and hug. Fathers and mothers tend to make physical contact with their children in different ways. Fathers tend to roughhouse more, while moms tend to cuddle more. We also know that moms are more physical with their baby boys under six months of age than with their daughters under six months. On the other hand, they talk to and smile at their baby girls more than they do their boys.

There are reasons for this that take us beyond the scope of this book. But it's important for you as a new parent to realize that you react to your children differently based on their sex.

Talking with your infant children and touching them are both vital forms of contact. Make sure you're doing both. Just as your children need milk and food to stay alive, so they need your words and your touch to survive. If you talk to your child a lot, and if you hug, hold and handle her frequently, she senses your presence, your attention and your love.

Principle 5

**Express warmth and positive feelings
toward your child a hundred times a
day—through your words.**

This may sound like a slight exaggeration, but I
want to emphasize its importance. Many adults are
capable of handling and hugging their children, but
are not so good at expressing verbally their feelings
for their children. I hear all too frequently excuses
like this: "I'm not good at saying 'I love you.' When
I was a kid my folks never said those kinds of things
to me." So now these parents don't even bother
trying to say how much they love their children.
They simply blame their own parents for their inabil-
ity to express affection, and now they are going to
model for their children that same style of cool
distance.

This is not acceptable. Parents can learn to express positive feelings even if they aren't used to it.
Telling your child he is wonderful and lovable is not
an optional thing for parents. It isn't like deciding
whether going to Disney World would be good for

your children, and then deciding you can't afford to go. Telling your child how much you love him is as essential to his life as his daily milk. This isn't a discretionary activity. It is vital to the psychological survival of your child. There are no excuses for not expressing love, warmth and many, many compliments.

"Oh, but I don't want my child to get a big head," I hear occasionally. I say, "So what. Let him get a big head. A big head means he thinks well of himself. Isn't that better than him thinking he's worthless?"

Again, start as soon as that baby is born. Get used to telling him out loud that you love him, that he's special and he's beautiful. Here are some things children from one day to 18 years old need to hear frequently:

"I love you."
"I think you're a neat kid."
"You are gorgeous."
"I like doing things with you."
"I like being with you."
"I really like the way you...(fill in the missing blank with whatever behavior you like)."
"What a great job you did on...(fill in the blank)."

Get the idea? If you haven't been comfortable with making comments like these before parenting, then begin with your newborn child. It's pretty easy to say these things to a week-old child. She just looks back at you with admiration. If you keep telling her how lovable she is while she's an infant, she gets used to it and so do you. As she grows up it becomes a natural part of the way you communicate with her. And you'll notice it also becomes part of the way she communicates with you. Now that's delightful—to hear your daughter say: "Dad, I love you. It's really fun doing stuff with you."

What more reward can a parent receive?

Principle 6

**Set clear boundaries with your child
and stick with those boundaries.**

Small children don't have any sense of bound-aries. They don't have a clue as to where they end and someone else begins. So they hang on to Mom's pant's leg while she does the laundry, they put their hands in Dad's dinner as he's trying to eat it, and they bite their sister's arm when she isn't looking. They have no idea of the danger that lies in the spaces outside themselves—the edge of the staircase, the inside of the refrigerator or the mouth of the dog.

Everything is one big smear of reality. An essen-tial task of childhood is to learn to separate the various parts of reality. The first major separation for children is learning what is *them* and what is *not* them.

Children gradually need to develop what is called an *ego boundary*. This is a psychological line that is drawn around the self and separates the self from everything else. It's like a circle around the person. Everything inside that circle is the child. Everything outside that circle is not the child. It's that simple.

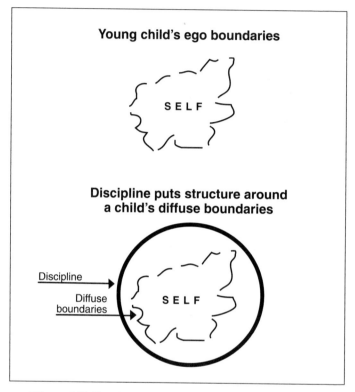

The child's feelings of hunger are inside the circle and so they are part of the child. The bottle of milk is outside her circle and so it is not the child. I know this all sounds obvious to you and me. But to a newborn child that boundary line is not yet drawn, so everything seems to be a part of the child. Children who never develop that ego boundary as they grow up live by the axiom: "What's yours is mine."

Your job as a new parent is to help your son or daughter develop an ego boundary. One way you do that is by saying "no." After your son has enough milk but stills wants more you say "no." And you mean it. You don't give him any more. When it's time to put him down for a nap and he fusses, you still put him down. You are saying "no" to his fussing. When he reaches for your hot coffee, you say "no" and move the coffee cup away. When he grabs the cat's tail, you say "no" and pull his hand away.

When you do these things you aren't simply being a "meany," nor are you merely keeping your son safe from harm. You are helping him establish his ego boundary, a very important task for a young child to accomplish.

You also help your child set good boundaries by not giving in to those sad little eyes that really want another cookie. Parents aren't usually very good at staying consistent. Children have a way of manipulating their parents so they get what they want. You may not like to see your child cry. You try to avoid her tears whenever they come. Whatever it takes from you to stop her crying, you'll do. If she cries you pick her up, feed her more, play with her longer, turn on her favorite television program, allow her to stay up an extra half hour. All because you aren't comfortable with her tears.

Certainly, when your child cries you want to be responsive to her needs. Crying is one of the few ways an infant can make her needs known. But other times a child cries because she wants something that's not good for her. At those times you need to say "no" and stick with it. This is the time not to give in to her tears.

You also set clear boundaries for your children when you define for them what they can and cannot do. You don't need to do this for newborn infants, of course. But once they begin moving around, you must begin setting rules. At first, the rules apply to issues of safety: "You can't tease the dog; you must stay away from the road; you can't get too close to the stairs." A little later you add other rules for the health and well-being of your child: "You can have only juice before bedtime; you must sleep in your own bed; you can't hit your sister; you must eat all the food on your plate."

Once these rules are set, you need to stick to them. Too many parents set rules and then don't enforce them. Their children grow up knowing that rules and boundaries don't matter, so they think they can do pretty much whatever they want. "What's yours is mine" and "I'll do as I darn well please."

As you begin your journey into parenting, please set a goal to help your child establish clear and distinct ego boundaries. You do that by setting precise boundaries with your child right from the beginning. "No" means no. The rules you set should be clear and simple. Then enforce them gently. Don't back away from your rules and give in because

"She's such a sweetie" or because you're too tired to argue.

I don't want this section to sound too harsh. I don't want you to become a rigid, overly serious parent who is simply into discipline, rules and structure. No. Enjoy your child. Be sensitive to your child's needs and respond to his or her real needs as best you can. But when you realize that something the child wants is not good for him or her, then say "no" and stick with it.

Decide early on what little rules you want to put in place to protect your child. Make sure you say those rules to your child and then follow through with your insistence that the rules be obeyed. Love your child by saying "yes" when you recognize a real need; and love her by saying "no" when your child's need or behavior leads to harm.

Principle 7

**Do not engage in physical or verbal
violence with your children.**

This principle seems obvious, doesn't it? There's
no way you'd ever strike your child. And certainly
you won't say anything hurtful to your child. Even
thinking about it makes you sad. But let me tell you
about Gloria.

Gloria was 23 when she married. Shortly afterward she became pregnant. As the time approached
for her baby's birth, she thought a lot about being a
good parent. She had been spanked frequently as a
child and her parents used to needle her about being
overweight. She promised herself that she would
never strike her child, nor would she ever criticize
him in a demeaning way.

Jason was born healthy and lively. The first
months were delightful. He could do no wrong. By
seven months, though, he began to crawl and get into
places he shouldn't be. Gloria kept her promise at
first. She told herself to remain calm and breathe
deeply when she was forever pulling Jason from
troublesome spots. By the end of her first year of

parenting, Gloria was getting a little frayed around the edges. Jason was always into something or always under her feet. She felt she could do nothing else during the day but watch him and keep him out of trouble. Frustration was mounting. She was becoming annoyed with his antics. She was losing patience.

One day after he had gotten into the cabinet under the sink and dumped the wastebasket all over the kitchen floor, Gloria lost it. She grabbed him roughly by the arm, slapped his hand hard four times, yanked him away from the mess with a solid swat to his behind and yelled at him, "You are a very bad boy. Get the hell out of my sight."

She had done the very thing she promised herself she wouldn't do. By the time she cleaned up the mess, she felt guilty, went to Jason, cuddled him and told him she was sorry and she wouldn't do that again. But she did. Her frustrations kept turning to anger. And her anger got expressed in hitting and yelling.

What happened here? Gloria had such good intentions prior to Jason's birth. Good intentions are not enough. When a person gets into a stressful situation she tends to regress. She becomes more primitive in her responses. She forgets the promises she made to herself and reaches for whatever behavior might work in the situation. The behavior most deeply imprinted in her is that of her parents. The way they treated her becomes the way she acts when the stress is intense. In this case, Gloria's parents spanked her frequently and called her names. Now when Gloria has "had it" with Jason, she forgets about her promises and looks for behaviors that stop him from annoying her. She reaches into her grab bag of strategies and pulls out the one most familiar to her—the way her parents did it.

So what can you do to avoid physical or verbal violence with your children? Well, a number of things:

1. **Make a commitment to non-violence—as Gloria did.**

To make this more than empty thoughts and words, you need to spend time within yourself encouraging this commitment to take root. You need to think about this child coming into the world. He or she is your responsibility. You want this child to grow up and live a full human life. You want him or her to have good self-esteem and a high level of confidence. One way of making sure that happens is by building up that child verbally and touching that child lovingly.

2. **Respect your child as you would an adult.**

This child is not your property to do with as you please. No, he belongs to himself. If you would not hit an adult for misbehavior, then don't hit your child. Realize that a child's job in life is to explore things—to find out what's inside a garbage pail, to eat the cat's food and to see how far he can throw the mashed carrots. You may not enjoy these explorations, especially after your own hard day, but try to understand that your child is doing precisely what he's supposed to be doing.

3. De-dramatize your thinking.

When Jason dumps out the garbage on the kitchen floor, it's not the same as your father having a heart attack. When Jason throws carrot strikes at the wall, it's not as terrible as your sister being in a serious car accident. When Jason pees on the new carpet, it doesn't fall in the same category of catastrophe as your best friend being laid off from her job.

Try to keep a relaxed perspective. Almost all of the things Jason does in the first years of his life will become stories to laugh at when the family history is told. Try laughing at them now as well as later on. Realize that the things he does now may be annoying at times, but they are not "awful, catastrophic, terrible, dreadful, horrible, ghastly or horrid." They are unpleasant and slightly annoying, that's all.

4. Either go away from your child or go closer in stressful times.

When your child does something annoying, you may need a moment to catch your breath, slow down and get calm before responding to her. If you need that moment, then take it. Go away either physically or psychologically. Step into the bathroom and take a drink of water before you respond to the situation. If you can't do that because your child let the dog out of the yard and you can't delay chasing after it, then try to get away psychologically. By that I mean concentrate on chasing the dog. Don't let yourself think about how you're going to give your daughter hell when you get back home. Just get the dog back. Once the dog is home safe, sound and delighted that he had a moment's freedom, then you can address your daughter. But by then you will have put some space between you and her, and now you can respond more calmly.

When I talk about going away, I'm talking about *you* going away from your child momentarily. Often, parents try getting space by pushing their child away. That's when you can get violent. Do not push your child away in times of stress, although that's a very natural thing to do. If something stresses you, your first instinct is to get it out of your way. If a mosquito keeps bothering you, you try to push it away, usually by killing it. Only when you can't kill all the mosquitoes do you then go away. You go into the house.

With your child you need to think differently. When you're stressed by your child's behavior, then you go away for a moment. Don't push your child away.

5. Decide to never spank your child.

This rule may be somewhat controversial. There are valid opinions on both sides of this issue. But I'm saying to you it's best to start off with the attitude, "I don't need to use spanking to help my child set boundaries and learn responsibility. There are other methods that are more successful and will show more respect for the child."

If your belief is that you will never strike your child, then you will always be looking for other forms of discipline. Thinking this way makes you more creative in the way you respond to your child. You can get through your years of parenting without ever spanking your children, yet you can help them form their ego boundaries and develop a strong sense of responsibility. In fact, I believe you have a better chance of your children becoming responsible if you don't spank.

Responsibility is learned by children experiencing the natural consequences of their behavior. Spanking is rarely the natural consequence of behavior. By taking away a toy your child is abusing, by separating him from his sister when he is hitting her, by taking away food he is throwing at the dog, you teach your child what happens when he or she misbehaves. If the consequences are painful enough, then your son or daughter learns how to better deal with the object or situation. That's learning responsibility.

Hitting a child is a serious invasion of that child's boundaries. By doing so you contradict one of your parenting goals—namely to help a child develop good ego boundaries. Although you're teaching your child to set clear ego boundaries, by hitting your child you arbitrarily cross those boundaries and invade his or her space.

I hope this all makes sense to you, and you begin your parenting career by resolving not to strike your children ever. Decide to respect their boundaries just as you would those of a stranger on the street or any other adult. By the time your children grow up and leave home, I hope you can say, "I have never hit my children." That would truly be a statement of respect and honor toward your children.

Principle 8

**Realize your child is a fragile but
sacred human person.**

As you hold your eight-pound baby for the first time, you know just how fragile she is. You also sense with awe the holiness of human life. You handle your daughter so gently. Everything you do with her and around her is done with care, love and patience as though you were setting an expensive raw diamond in a gold ring.

It is absolutely critical that you maintain that attitude throughout your parenting life with your child. As she grows up she may not appear so fragile or so sacred. But she is. Inside, your child is still a child. The life force you once saw as sacred remains sacred always. You cannot ever let yourself forget that you have been entrusted with this fragile, sacred human life, and you must treat her so always.

When a parent abuses a child he or she damages the spirit of the child. The sacred life of that child is defiled. That tender, fragile and delicate life source is permanently scarred. This is not a simple matter of:

"Oh, Daddy lost his temper. Everything's all right now."

No, your child—whether she is three months, three years or 13 years—is a delicate spirit and needs to be handled with gentle, loving care.

I have seen too much child abuse in my lifetime. I have listened to the reports of sexual and physical onslaughts perpetrated against children. I have heard parents in parking lots and at grocery stores verbally abuse their children. These people have lost sight of the fragile and sacred person entrusted to their care.

Starting out as a parent, you can help stop the abuse. But do it positively by realizing your child is delicate and is sacred. You have no right to invade the personal space of this child physically, sexually or verbally. Your duty is to protect the sacredness of your child and to support and give growth to the beautiful life form that is entrusted into your care. Please respect your child always, no matter how she may seem to misbehave.

And know how vulnerable and tender your child is. Always be gentle. Love her graciously and with a very soft touch.

Principle 9

Feed your child healthful food and avoid junk food as best as you can.

This also may seem obvious to you as you think about this precious life about to be born. You may be determined to give your child only vegetables, fruits, fiber and carbohydrates. You're committed to not using candy and sugar as snacks or as ways to keep your child quiet.

But it will be very tough for you to keep your resolve. There is so much sugar out there that you won't be able to avoid feeding it to your son or daughter. I saw a striking statistic a while ago that said the average amount of sugar consumed by *every* American is 160 pounds per year. Think of it! Your child will be consuming more than her body weight every year, possibly for her entire life. Every can of regular soda contains upwards of 12 teaspoons of sugar. And we know that kids drink more soda than milk.

Sugar makes the pancreas work hard. Too much sugar makes the pancreas work *too* hard. You can easily destroy an overworked pancreas. The pancreas makes insulin. If a ruined pancreas can't make enough insulin, you set the stage for diabetes. Diabetes is fast becoming a major health problem in the United States.

When you buy baby food, read the labels. Pay attention to how much sugar or artificial flavorings have been added. Manufacturers often increase the amount of sugar and salt in baby food so that when Mom or Dad test it, it tastes good to them. Babies aren't as fussy. Their taste buds aren't as acute as adults. They don't need such strong flavors. So look for foods low in sugar and salt.

The authors of the *Tufts University Guide to Total Nutrition* explain: "In most cases, the less sugar, corn syrup, starch, modified food starch, and added flour, the more nutrients you get for the calories. The problem isn't that these ingredients are harmful to your baby; it's more a matter of not 'spending' calories on extra ingredients that are not nourishing."

Although you want to be careful about children's eating habits, you don't want to deny them what their bodies need. While fats and cholesterol often need to be restricted in adult diets, the same is not so true for children under the age of two. Children without sufficient fats and calories can have problems in body cell formation and develop problems with proper growth.

Don't overdo your focus on your child's eating. Attend to serving healthful food and watch mainly for sugar and salt content. As your children get older avoid junk foods with them as well as you can. Try not to use candy, chips and Twinkies as rewards or incentives to stop crying or to behave. Instead, use hugs and kisses (not chocolate ones).

Try to get into a pattern of eating regularly with your children. By that I mean there should be set times when children eat. They eat at meal times and then at regularly planned snack times. Not in between. You don't want your children to learn to eat all day long any old time. By waiting for certain times, you teach children a little discipline and help them gain a better sense of boundaries. Many adult diet plans recommend eating only at meal times and not in between meals.

Again, pay attention to proper eating habits with your children, but don't become a fanatic about it. If you have a problem with eating in your own life and focus on it frequently, the same will probably happen to your child. Relax with this area of concern and be reasonable as well as watchful.

Principle 10

**Control the amount of television you
and your children watch.**

Television plays an important and influential role in the life of your child. You notice something extraordinary happening by the time your child is six or seven months old. He is lying on the floor in the living room playing with you. The television is on in the background. He isn't paying any attention to it. All of a sudden a commercial comes on, he stops what he's doing and turns his head toward the screen. He watches the commercial. When it's ended, he returns to his play with you.

I couldn't believe it when my children did this. What incredible power exists in that box. Colors, sounds, quick actions all stimulated my children's senses. The messages about every material object imaginable were already seeping into their innocent and uncluttered minds.

Certainly, there are some great programs on television for children. Allowing your son to watch those is fine. "Mr. Rogers Neighborhood" and

"Sesame Street" remain outstanding children's pro-grams. But watching a lot of cartoons, interspersed with commercials about toys and cereals, is not helpful to children.

Statistics on this vary, but it appears that children watch between four and six hours of television a day. I fear for their minds. Television is passive entertain-ment. Your son need not do anything but sit and take in the action before him. He doesn't have to develop his own imagination and his own creative skills. Furthermore, sitting four to six hours a day is not good for his body, which was created to move. The human body works best if it moves regularly and with some vigor. Television encourages the very opposite.

Another caution with television: Try not to use it as a baby-sitter. You have supper to make or the wash to do. Baby Danny is clinging to your kneecap like he's part of your body. So you set him in front of the television as a way of getting him extricated from your knee and freeing you to do your work. It's understandable that you want to do that, but try to resist the temptation, unless the program is one you have decided is good for him to watch. Sometimes try to plan your work when a worthwhile program is on. However, be sure to watch some of the good children's programs *with* your son. It's a great time for bonding and teaching your child new things.

As your child gets a little older, attempt to restrict television to certain times during the day. Be structured about this. Allow him to watch certain programs. Then when those programs are over, television goes off. Obviously this has considerable implications for you as a parent. You have to spend more of your time entertaining and playing with your child rather than having television do it. You have to do more reading to your child, which is much more beneficial to him than watching television anyway.

If you as an adult watch a lot of television, you need to change your habits as well. By sitting in front of the entertainment box every night from 7 to 10 o'clock, you almost guarantee that your child will do the same as he grows up. Television-watching deadens family relationships. You're all there in the same room, but you're involved with the box, not with each other. As a marriage counselor, I have seen hundreds of couples whose relationships have been damaged, in part due to one partner watching television for hours every night. Television doesn't teach your child social skills. He learns those from direct interaction with you.

So pay attention to the secret enemy that has infiltrated almost every household in the United States—television. Focus on active participation in your son's life through reading, playing, talking and active caring.

Chapter 4

Principles and Tools for Taking Care of Yourself

When that first "gift of life" cries and coos its way into your heart, you give yourself over to her fully. She is gorgeous, wonderful and precious. She occupies your every thought and feeling. You're going to be the best Mom or Dad, and she will be the best little girl. You nurture her, respond to her every need, morning, noon and night, and care for her as you have never cared for someone before.

How wonderful! Here you are, loving a newborn child, knowing you are responsible for her, realizing she depends totally on you! These awarenesses free you from self-centered thoughts and feelings. You focus totally on her and love her unconditionally.

You don't ask her for any love in return. You simply give without looking to receive. The love you have for your newborn child is as close to altruistic loving as you will ever come. Enjoy it, but....

From the beginning I want you to be sure to take care of yourself and your personal needs as well. New parents, to their own detriment, often neglect themselves and their adult relationships. If you don't take care of yourself and the other aspects of your life, not only do you hurt yourself, but you eventually become a less effective parent. So what do you need to do to take care of yourself and the other aspects of your life?

Principle 11

Understand and manage your own feelings.

Becoming a parent opens you to the full range of human emotions. Right now you feel anticipation, excitement, anxiety, uncertainty, glee and fulfillment. Once your child comes, you will feel, along with the above, every other possible human emotion—deep love, tenderness, worry, anger, sadness, guilt, resentment, pride, satisfaction. You need to know what to do with these feelings when they come to you.

Most parents never consider their own feelings and what to do with them as part of parenting. You need to ask: What are my feelings? Do my feelings help or hurt me and my child? How do I change those that hurt? And how can I express all my feelings in ways that help my child and me feel comfortable and secure?

1. What are my feelings?

Once your baby comes home from the hospital, the whirlwind begins. You're feeding this precious child, cooking for her, changing her diapers, cleaning her, carrying and cuddling her. You don't have time to have feelings. You just keep moving. But the feelings are there. You're just not paying attention at the moment.

One evening after you put your daughter to sleep and sit down in a state of deep fatigue, tears start rolling down your cheeks. Where in the world are those coming from, you wonder. You're so happy. You're a mother. Your dream has come true. You love your darling child. So why the tears?

Stress! Think about it for a second. Your body just went through a very traumatic experience. It's not used to carrying around a nine-pound child on the inside. Nor is it used to delivering such a child. So your body is worn out. But you come home and immediately start caring for your child. You're up through the night. You catch a nap while she sleeps during the day. You have no clue as to what you're doing with your new daughter. So you worry, feel unsure and are forever calling your own mother or a friend to figure out what to do next.

Everything in your life has just changed dramatically. It catches up with you. You sit down and in your tears release all that stress. Good for you.

Feelings are coursing through your body and soul all the time. Much of the time you simply don't pay any attention to them. You just go on doing the stuff of life. After you have a baby, more feelings and stronger feelings circulate through your psychological system. Again, because you're so busy loving and caring for your child, you may not stop to notice all the feelings.

I want you to begin now to stop and pay very close attention to your feelings. You might want to keep a diary record of your thoughts and feelings as you await your child's birth. Take time every day to write down your feelings about what is happening to your body, what it feels like to carry this life within you, what you anticipate once baby comes, and so on. Don't censor your feelings, thinking you can only have warm and cuddly feelings. No, you're experiencing the full range from comfortable to uncomfortable.

Feelings are neither good nor bad. They have no morality. They are just there, part of you, giving you some signals about what's going on inside of you. So let them come as they will. If you have a regretful feeling, for example, let it be there. You may be feeling sad because you didn't plan this baby and she's coming before you really wanted a child. Write down that thought and feeling. You're not going to be a bad mother because you feel moments of regret.

Or you may be having doubts. You might be wondering if this was such a good idea. You might be feeling selfish, realizing you have to give up a lot to have a child. Fine. Feel those things. Think about them, write them down. Say "yes" to them. They are simply feelings.

When the excitement comes and the warm glow floods your heart, stop and relish those feelings too. Let yourself feel the love and tenderness you already experience. And write it down. Pause during your pregnancy and befriend your emotions. Identify them and give them names. Tell them to your partner or to a friend. And write them down. If you start doing this now, then when your child comes you will more likely pause, enjoy and embrace the emotions you feel.

2. Do your feelings help or hurt you or your child?

Remember I just said feelings are neither good nor bad. They are not right or wrong. But they are often either helpful or hurtful in particular situations. A nurturing feeling toward your child is obviously helpful to him. An angry feeling toward your son may be hurtful to him. A contented feeling when you look at him sleeping in his bed is helpful to you. A guilty feeling that puts you down as a parent is hurtful to you.

Evaluate your feelings, then, on whether they are helpful, useful or productive on the one hand, or whether they are hurtful, not useful or unproductive on the other hand. Don't think of them as good or bad, right or wrong, or even as appropriate or inappropriate. They are just feelings and can work for you or against you or others. You want your feelings to work for your good and the good of your child.

3. How can you change those feelings that are hurtful?

This could be a book in itself. In fact, it is. To learn more about how to change feelings that don't work for you, please read my book *Thinking Reasonably* in the Life Skills Series of books.

As you begin your parenting career, realize one thing that makes a huge difference in the way you treat your child and yourself. *You create your own feelings.* That's right. Your child does not make you angry or sad. Your child doesn't make you proud or excited. You make yourself feel those things. You create your own feelings. No one else has that much power in your life that they can make you feel something. No. You generate your own feelings. I know it seems as if other people *make* you have certain feelings. But I want you to challenge that belief right now.

Let's say your child cries through the night every night for the first month. By the end of that month, you might become very annoyed by the sound of her wailing. At 4 o'clock in the morning, when you haven't yet gotten any sleep, you're irritated by the whining child. Does she make you irritated? No. Certainly, she has to be crying in order for you to irritate yourself, but she is not the cause of your irritation. So what is, you wonder? Your thoughts are the cause of your irritation.

That's right. Your thoughts create your irritation, not your baby's crying. As you're crawling out of bed at 4 in the morning, you're thinking: "What the heck is the matter with her? By now, she should be sleeping through the night. Most babies are. What luck, we get the one baby who never needs to sleep. I have to get my rest. I'll be a mess the rest of this day." These kinds of thoughts create the irritation—not the fact that your baby is crying.

Imagine the same scene, but different thoughts as you stumble out of bed. You wouldn't get irritated if you thought: "Oh, something must be wrong with baby. But it's good she's crying. That means she's alive and kicking. The one thing that scares me is her dying in her sleep." Different thoughts, different feelings. Since your thoughts create your feelings, you try to change your thinking if you want to change your feelings, right? It's so important to realize that *you* create your feelings because then you gain the power to change your feelings by changing your thinking.

Think in loving ways and you have loving feelings. Think positive thoughts and you have optimistic feelings. Think joyful thoughts about the future and you have excited feelings. On the other hand, think demanding thoughts and you feel anger. Think catastrophic thoughts about the future and you're filled with anxiety and worry. Think negative thoughts and you feel sad and down.

Your thinking is under your control. Challenge those thoughts that lead to hurtful and unproductive feelings. Try to change your thinking. Realize that just because you believe something to be true does not make it true. When you have a feeling that doesn't work well for you, it's because you have unreasonable and inaccurate thoughts. Doubt your thoughts in that case, and change your thinking to more positive, less demanding and less catastrophic thoughts.

4. How can you express your feelings in ways that are helpful to your child and to you?

Generally, you need to *say* your feelings. Many parents rarely tell their children what they feel about anything, except what they are angry about. Parents want their children to tell them what's going on in their lives, but are unwilling to tell their children what's going on inside of them. Parents need to become much more self-revealing if they want their kids to grow up as self-revealing people.

Tell your feelings by making yourself the subject of the sentence. *I* feel sad, happy, angry, delighted. Don't just say: "That was a sweet birthday card you gave me." Say: "I feel so grateful to have a son like you who'd give me such a sweet card." The one emotion many parents have trouble expressing in a self-revealing way is anger. It's very easy to make your *child* the subject of the sentence instead of *you*.

Let's say your daughter knocks a cup of milk to the floor and you get upset. You might say: "You are such a clumsy kid. Pay attention to what you're doing."

See, you're expressing your anger, making your *daughter* the subject of the sentence. Turn that a little and make *you* the subject of the sentence: "I get so annoyed with you when you do things like that. It really bothers me because I have to clean it up." That's a very healthy way of expressing anger. For many years now, this approach to expressing yourself has been called making "I" statements rather than "you" statements.

Allow your feelings to be whatever they are; decide which ones work for you and your child and which work against you; think differently to change the feelings that are unproductive; and express your feelings by making "I" the subject of the sentence.

Principle 12

Keep your marriage a priority.

Once you have a child, you toss another ball into your juggling routine. You then have your marriage partner, your job or career, your home, your relatives and friends, and baby. Your baby will take up the majority of your time. The other aspects of your life have to adjust to the baby. One of the easiest balls to drop if you have too many in the air at once is your marriage. You can't quit working. You can't slack off on the washing, ironing, scrubbing and cooking. But you can take your marriage partner for granted, trusting that he or she will be there as needed.

For now, it's hard to give much attention to that relationship. So the marriage can fall into a corner of the closet. It's there like a pair of good, but old, shoes that get worn once in a while, only to be dropped back in the closet after the nice evening out.

New fathers sense the shift in priority as Mom attaches to the baby. Often, men feel some rejection by their wives when the first baby arrives. They experience a wave of jealousy, because before the baby arrived they had an exclusive relationship with their wives. Now, this little creature absorbs all of Mom's time and attention. Fathers feel a twinge of sadness, a sense of losing their wives to their children. Fortunately, fathers get over this feeling quickly. They realize their wives can love their children and them at the same time. Loving one doesn't mean not loving the other.

Having a baby adds another whole layer of busyness to a marriage. The couple doesn't have as much time with each other. They feel tired in the evening because they have been up every night for the past week or month. Their communication with each other can drop off. Their fun time together can diminish. Nights out and late Saturday morning love-making can no longer happen spontaneously. Baby's presence changes their relationship.

I want you to be aware of the change that takes place in your marital relationship. I don't want to paint too bleak a picture. Many couples bond even better after the birth of their child. They share the moments of delight when baby coos or smiles. They worry together about baby getting enough food, being sick, and not having an outburst in church. But the relationship changes and in many ways it becomes more difficult to spend time together and share deeply with one another.

So you need to prepare in advance. Be ready for

the changes that baby's presence will have on you and your relationship. Commit yourself to one another and to keeping your marriage a top priority. Profess your love for each other more frequently so you remain conscious of your commitment and care for each other. Remember, you are partners in this project of raising a child. This isn't one parent's work while the other gets involved in career or house or relatives.

Partners work together, laugh together, cry together, worry together and love together. Your child can bring you closer to each other or can drive you apart from each other. For you to come closer, you need to remain conscious of the fact that you are partners. You love each other. You're in this together. Your work each day isn't finished until both of you are finished. You both take your turns getting up in the middle of the night to care for your child. You both know when the doctor's appointments are and how to contact the diaper service. You both can make baby's formula and change his diapers after they have been affected by that formula. You're in this together. Commit yourselves to coming together and parenting this child as equal partners. That approach will keep your relationship strong.

Single parents reading this may feel sad and alone because there isn't anyone there to help them or to be close. Being a single parent is perhaps one of the most difficult jobs in the world, not just because you have to earn income and care for children and home, but because you're alone in the process.

Maintaining your close friendships with other adults becomes critical for single parents. I know it feels as though you have no time to engage in such luxuries as lunch out on a Saturday afternoon or an evening movie with a neighbor, but your efforts to remain connected to your adult friends will benefit you immensely. Try not to forget about your friends because your baby demands so much of your time and attention. You need adult contact.

Without it, parenting becomes a tremendous burden carried alone through uncharted territory.

Principle 13

**Get out of the house once a week with
your partner or friend.**

Please take this principle to heart. I was going to
tuck it into the previous principle about keeping your
marriage or friendship a priority. It fits there. But it's
such an important, practical thing to do, I want to
make it a principle by itself.

When you first bring your baby home, you may
not want to go out and leave her with your parents or
a baby-sitter. Okay, I'll give you the first month or
so. You might not feel the need to get away. But after
that, it's important that you get out with your partner
or a friend.

Ask your parents or a trusted sibling to baby-sit
the first time, if possible. You won't worry as much
when you leave if your parents are caring for your
baby.

Then get out together, even for a short time. Eat
dinner at a fast-food restaurant, have breakfast at a
24-hour eatery, walk through a mall. It need not be
an expensive, lengthy night out. Just get out together—talk, share, laugh together.

Then, get in the habit of doing this every week. Once a week, the two of you (if you're married *just the two of you*) arrange to get out of the house and be together.

But that could get expensive, you think. Baby-sitters don't come cheap any more. Think of it this way. If you own your own house, you buy fertilizer a couple of times a year to put on your lawn. What's more important, a perfectly weed-free lawn or a close, loving marriage? Cut out a couple of beers each week, a couple of packs of cigarettes, or the five cups of coffee you drink daily, and put that money into your baby-sitting fund. This is an issue of priority. Your marriage or your adult friendships are so important in themselves and are vital for the growth and development of your child that you need to invest in them.

One of the best, easiest and most enjoyable investments you can make in your marriage or your friendship is to get out of the house once a week with your partner or friend. Please do yourselves and your child a great favor by taking my advice here. I have a little warning for you. As your child or children get older you will find you have less and less time with each other. Believe it or not, your children demand more time of you as they grow up. So seize the opportunity now to get away regularly. It will make you better partners and friends.

Principle 14

Engage in and maintain other aspects of your life.

Don't become only a mom or a dad. Make sure you remain invested in all the other stuff life offers. Certainly you have to make adjustments in the amount of time you can give to bowling or golf or sewing or shopping. But don't sacrifice those things altogether.

Moms have a little more trouble with this principle than do dads. Moms are usually more involved with the new baby. You've created and carried this little guy for nine months already. It's not as though your relationship just started with your child the day he was born. You've been relating nearly a year before he came out and said hello.

Moms, then, tend to invest all their emotional and psychic energy in this child. That's great in one sense. It's a truly loving act. But be careful not to over-invest to the detriment of losing a sense of balance and fullness in your own life.

Here are a couple of things you can do to help yourself remain a well-rounded (I probably shouldn't use that term for a mother trying to regain her shape after delivery) and balanced person:

1. Take time for yourself each day.

When my wife was first pregnant with our son, Andy, she read something most helpful to her. The writer said that every mother, especially of a new-born child, should do something just for herself once a day. That might be to take a walk, do your nails, soak in a bathtub, read a book.

Indulge yourself in a way that is satisfying and fulfilling to you. It can't be something you do for someone else. It has to be something that fills you up, not drains you out.

2. Try to maintain an interest you had before Baby.

Once Baby comes it's very easy to stop doing things you used to enjoy. You just don't have time, you think. Or, you might feel selfish if you want to read instead of playing with your baby 16 hours a day. No, it's very important for you to maintain your adult interests.

If you enjoyed reading politics, then make time to continue doing so. If you always liked piecing together jig-saw puzzles, then buy one, set it up on the card table and do it when you can. It may take longer than before you had a baby, but you'll still enjoy it and gain some needed space from your baby and all that mothering activity.

3. Realize you are more than a mom or a dad.

You are a multifaceted human being. Although most of your psychic energy is directed toward your baby in those first days and months, you need to realize you are still more than a parent. I'm sure you can sense the message in these last several principles: You need to keep balance in your life. The presence of a baby can easily knock your life off center. Try to remain grounded in your total reality.

After Baby, you continue to be a marriage partner, a homemaker, an active member of the work force, an extended family member, a friend to a circle of people, a volunteer at the hospital or church, and a self-contained, reflective person who needs his or her time and space.

I want you to keep your perspective. Don't see your baby as your total life. Mothers who remain home with their children quickly learn that their children cannot be their only focus. By the end of the day, they crave adult conversation. They need feedback from a more intelligent life form. They would kill for a conversation about politics or clothes or movies or talk shows. The bottom line is this:

You are not your babies. You are more than a parent. Don't let go of all those other aspects of your life.

Principle 15

Get rest and physical exercise.

You go to the hospital in pain. You work very hard—sometimes for many hours. You deliver a gift to the world. You sleep a little, feel uncomfortable, learn how to feed a baby and are sent home. All within two days. When you get home, the baby cries and you want to jump and respond. There is so much to do at home—prepare the baby's room, wash clothes, write thank you notes, call friends, and take care of your parents and in-laws who want to come over and help. You know you're supposed to rest, but there just isn't any time.

Wait. Stop. You absolutely need to rest. Let as much work go at first as possible. You need to realize your body has just gone through a major trauma. It has been seriously weakened by the wonderful, but very difficult, process of birthing your child.

In the past, mothers used to stay in the hospital four days before going home. The only reason that has changed to two days is because insurance companies don't want to pay for four days. They want to pay for only two days. From a medical or health perspective, four days in the hospital allows the mother to recuperate from the birth. It allows her to catch her breath and slowly ease into parenting.

Somehow, most moms think that once they are discharged from the hospital, they are in perfect shape. People who go into the hospital for "day surgery" come out in the late afternoon and think they can resume all the activities they engaged in the day before surgery. It ain't so. You may think giving birth is sort of like having day surgery. You should be able to go in, have the baby, come home, and be up and running without losing a beat.

Well, your body is crying "No, no, no!" It needs rest. It needs to recuperate. It needs to be pampered. So please, take it easy when you come home. Go slowly. Don't try to become "Super Mom" right away.

After you have rested for days, or weeks if need be, gradually try to get physical exercise. More than anything else, exercise helps you regain your physical strength and shape. It also serves as a therapeutic way to relax and drain off the tension and anxiety that a young parent experiences.

Start with a walk around the block. Just moving your body in the fresh air feels good and helps to restore your spirit, mind and body. Of course, if you go for a walk, you'll want to take your baby with you.

That's fine. But if you discover that you're more tense when you return because your baby fussed all through the walk, then you may need to wait for your partner or a friend to watch the baby while you take a solitary walk to refresh yourself.

Gradually you can increase your exercise as you feel stronger. One of the other benefits of doing exercise is that it begins showing your child right from the beginning how to live life. The human body was not made to sit around. It was created to move and move vigorously. If your child grows up in an atmosphere of physical action, he or she will learn that such activity is normal and part of everyday living.

It's never too early to begin modeling healthy behavior for your child.

Principle 16

Start now saving money for your child's college education.

Eighteen years may seem far away. And in some ways it is. However, before you know it your baby Jason will be going to preschool, then kindergarten, elementary school and junior high. All of a sudden he will be a senior in high school talking about where he wants to go to college. That's when you'll say, "I can't believe how fast the years have gone by. Our little baby is going off to college."

If he goes away to college, expect to pay between $15,000 and $20,000 per year for a state university in your state. If he wants to go anywhere else, you could be doubling or tripling that amount. Eighteen years from now, a college education at a state university will cost over $100,000. You'd better start saving your dollars.

By starting a savings program now you do a couple of important things. First of all, you get into a disciplined way of handling money. The amount you set aside every month is like a bill you're paying.

It has to be paid. You do it automatically. You never make an exception. Second, by starting now, you get the most benefit from the interest generated by your investment. Money is made from money. Your money will make a lot more money for you over 18 years than over 10 years or five years. So start now. Decide what you can put away and do so, month after month. When you feel you can increase that amount, do it. Try to not ever decrease that amount.

Your sacrifices at times might feel great. But you are preparing for your child's future as best you can. Even so, you may not be able to completely fund your child's college education. He might have to take out student loans, get a job on campus in a work-study program, or start saving himself from early on in his life. That's fine. There isn't any law that says you must supply your child with a total college education. If you can do so, that's a nice gift to give your child. However, it is a gift. It isn't an obligation or duty of parenting.

So I don't want you to feel guilty if you simply cannot afford to finance a college education. Do what you can to help. But start now!

Principle 17

**Work outside the home if you want to
or need to.**

For fathers as well as mothers, take as much time at home with your baby as you possibly can. Then go back to work if you want to or have to. Many first time mothers fret about leaving their babies with "someone else." They worry about issues of abandonment and separation anxiety. They wonder if they are cheating their babies out of an essential ingredient in a child's life—namely their own physical presence.

The reality of our lives today is that the majority of new mothers must work outside the home. So it may be a moot question to consider whether or not it's better for moms or dads to be home with the child all the time. If you have to work outside the home, try to let go of any guilt you have for not staying home. You are doing the best you can. That's all there is to it.

Realize that the key to being an effective parent is your ability to love your child. You might not be able to be near your child all day long, but when you are you can give her all the love you have.

If you can stay home, great. There is nothing that can replace the presence and love of the active parent who is always present to the child in those early days and years. In our society that arrangement is becoming more and more a luxury. But if you can do it, then go for it. It is most helpful to your child.

But what about you? Is it better for you to stay home or work outside the home? Well, in the short run, staying home is fine. It might feel like a breath of fresh air for you, and give you a nice change of pace in your life. But in the long run, mothers who remain at home tend to be less satisfied with their lives and more depressed than women who return to the work world. Women who remain home feel more isolated and out of life's mainstream. Many become more bored with life and dissatisfied with parenting as a full-time job.

Women in the work force gain a better balance in their lives. Parenting is not the only focus for them. They maintain another, very adult world and appreciate being able to move between work and parenting. That's not to say that parents who do both don't have a lot of stress and strain. They do. Sometimes the demands of work and home can be heavy. Nonetheless, having both seems to be more fulfilling and satisfying for most people.

The point I want to emphasize here is to relax with the decision you make of whether or not to work outside the home. If you have to do it, your child won't be scarred for life. Just love her when you're with her.

If you can stay home for a period of time, that would be good for the child, but it's not essential. Eventually, getting a job or career outside the home will probably lead to higher levels of personal satisfaction than staying at home.

Chapter 5
Parenting Partners

No doubt the reason it takes a man and a woman to create a child is because it takes more than one person to raise a child well. If it took two to create, it certainly takes at least two to parent. Single moms or dads have a tough time going it alone. They need support, encouragement, advice, relief—all of which can be given by a partner or a close friend or family member.

In a marriage or a partnership, that support is usually built in. The two people work at parenting together. An unmarried parent needs to find that support and relief from family or friends. In a coupled relationship, parenting a child can bring you to-gether or drive you apart. It brings you together if both of you are excited about the baby coming in the first place. In this case you are probably both reading the books and articles waiting for your baby's arrival. You attend pre-natal classes together, buy furniture and clothing together, and dream together about life with your child.

After your baby's birth, you both care for him, take turns getting up in the middle of the night, both change diapers and make formula and feed squashed carrots and clean up the table, floor and walls after feeding. You worry together about his health; you celebrate together his first smile as well as his first solid stool. In this scenario you come together. You parent your child as a team.

On the other hand, you might become more distant because you separate over the child. Perhaps one of you didn't even want the child. Or when Baby comes, you, the father, think the mother should get up in the night since she has to feed the baby anyway. Or you don't like changing diapers, and disappear when Baby needs help. You might not be around to see your baby's first smile, so you can't really celebrate together the significant events in this tiny baby's life. In this situation, the arrival of the baby can separate you as parents.

Whether you're married or not it's important to stay close to someone in the parenting of your child. In marriage both of you are equal parents. Your child needs both of you right from the beginning. She needs your warmth and tenderness, as well as your strength and nurturing love. Try to break any stereotypes you might have about what mothers are supposed to do for their children and what fathers are supposed to do. The parents who work best as a team have no stereotypes. They each do *whatever* is needed *when* it's needed. In fact, they anticipate what the other parent needs as well.

In other words, the father realizes how tired the mother is when Baby cries in the middle of the night, so he tells her to stay in bed and he will bring the baby to her for feeding. Mother anticipates Dad's need to get some paperwork done tonight, so she makes sure the child is quiet and out of Dad's path.

One of the best ways for new parents to come together as parents is by discussing beforehand the various aspects of bringing a child into the world. Discussing this book with one another will bring you together and help form you as a team in parenting your soon-arriving child. If you are a single mother, discussing this book with a close friend will help you feel more confident going into this journey of love.

How to use this book together

1. Read one principle at a time.

Make an appointment with each other in the evening or morning a couple of times a week. You can each read the section privately beforehand so you come prepared. Or you can read the section out loud to one another at your discussion time. Then discuss that principle—what it means, how you can implement it, what obstacles might arise that make it difficult to do, and so on.

2. **Make it a point when talking with other parents to ask them about the principles in this book.**

Let's say you have been discussing the principle regarding television watching for children. Ask other parents what they think about their children watching television, how they control television time, how much television they allow their children to watch, and so on. Then report to each other what other parents think on the subject. This will stimulate even further discussion on your part.

3. **Once your baby arrives, you can review with your partner how you're doing on these principles.**

It's a very good idea to have regular discussions—once a month—to evaluate your development as a parent. You can always return to this book and refresh yourself on the principles I've outlined.

Soon you will be a parent. Although I'm sure you have some anxiety over the delivery and birth—you don't know exactly what to expect even though you've had the classes—you're excited and impatient to see this little creature and become a parent. Without a doubt, becoming a parent has to be the greatest responsibility any human being can take on. Not only do you have the responsibility to keep this child safe and maintain her human life, but also you have the responsibility to develop, shape and direct a human person to become her very best self.

You have had little training to do such shaping and developing. Astronauts go to school and train for a long time before flying off into space. That's not half as important as your parenting your child. Attorneys spend three years in graduate school learning to function as lawyers. What they do cannot compare in importance to the work you do as a parent.

But your training has been mostly experiential. You were a kid once (maybe still feel like one). You watched your parents parent. You learned how they did it. You saw other kids' parents doing the parenting thing. You learned by seeing what they did. You watched television and saw how the Huxtables and the Simpsons did it. You learned. But none of that was enough.

That's why I'm glad you are reading this book, even though this, too, is not enough. But it does touch the important issues that you need to pay attention to as you begin this awesome responsibility. Keep this book close to you. Refer to it regularly. Keep reflecting on your parenting skills. Stop and talk with your partner and friends about what you're doing and how your child is growing. Keep on learning.

All professions demand continuing education. You need to demand that of yourself as a parent. Read, think, discuss, adapt, change, improve. As your child develops, you too need to develop as a parent.

Finally, love your child. Right now, before he or she arrives, that's not a message you may need to hear. But know throughout the life of your child that the best way to help him or her grow is by loving as fully as you can. Nothing can fill in the mistake holes you will make as a parent better than your love.

Good luck to you. May your child be well. May you have an easy delivery. And may you give your son or daughter all the love and tenderness needed for him or her to live a full and happy life.

Review of the Principles of Parenting

Principle 1

Communicate verbally with your child from day one and every day.

Principle 2

Avoid giving your child the silent treatment.

Principle 3

Realize that the relationship between you and your child is more important than any issue that separates you.

Principle 4

Be physical (gently, of course) with your children.

Principle 5

Express warmth and positive feelings toward your child a hundred times a day—through your words.

Principle 6

Set clear boundaries with your child and stick with those boundaries.

Principle 7

Do not engage in physical or verbal violence with your children.

Principle 8

Realize your child is a fragile but sacred human person.

Principle 9

Feed your child healthful food and avoid junk food as best as you can.

Principle 10

Control the amount of television you and your children watch.

Principle 11

Understand and manage your own feelings.

Principle 12

Keep your marriage a priority.

Principle 13

Get out of the house once a week with your partner or friend.

Principle 14

Engage in and maintain other aspects of your life.

Principle 15

Get rest and physical exercise.

Principle 16

Start now saving money for your child's college education.

Principle 17

Work outside the home if you want to or need to.

About the Author

Dale R. Olen, Ph.D., lives in Germantown, Wisconsin, with his wife, Joelyn, and their two children, Andy and Amy. Andy studies political science in college; Amy studies, works, and plays basketball in high school. They have a friendly beagle and an independent cat.

Dale received his doctorate in psychology from the University of Kansas in 1973. A year earlier he founded **The Justice and Peace Center** in Milwaukee, a social action organization attempting to create structural and societal change. During this time he realized that justice meant creating the opportunity for people to exercise their most basic right—namely, the right to live humanly. In his effort to understand what "living humanly" meant, he identified 14 "life skills" that fully alive people exhibit. He realized that his life's work was to help people develop these life skills so they could live full and happy lives. As a result, he started **Life Skills Center**, a mental health agency that he still directs today.

Dale teaches life skills through his writing, his lectures and workshops, and by doing psychotherapy. Since most people spend the majority of their time and energy at home and in work, he has concentrated his teaching in those two areas. He directs his life skills programs and materials toward families and businesses.

Dr. Olen is available for lectures and workshops on parenting and marriage, and he offers training programs for businesses. To invite Dr. Olen to speak with your group or to conduct a workshop, please call JODA Communications at 414-475-1600.

Index

119

Life Skills Parenting Series

The Thoughtful Art of Discipline

Here's the guide you need for parenting's tough times.

Certainly the most difficult aspect of parenting, discipline creates either responsible or defiant children. Dale Olen's insights and practical tools help to make discipline a positive and instructive experience for you and your children.

Dr. Olen shows you four approaches to discipline, starting with the use of authority to shape behavior; discussing ways you can change your reactions to misbehavior; explaining how to use logical consequences; and concluding with a "reverse psychology" approach called "paradoxical parenting."

Along with these methods, this book addresses your emotions as you discipline, especially anger. Once you control your upset and irritability, doing discipline leads gracefully to teaching responsibility to your children.

SPRING 1995 PUBLICATION:

Teaching Children to Like Themselves

Here's the book that answers the concern of almost every parent: "How can I help my child feel better about him or herself?"

In this easy-to-read book, Dale Olen reveals the causes of high and low self-esteem. He shows how children develop their sense of self and the role you play in that process. Then he describes the actions you need to take and the attitudes you can impart to your children to raise their self-images.

Through the pages of this book you sense the sacred core of your child's life. And you have the means to caress that life and give it growth.

Life Skills Parenting Series, *continued*

FALL 1995 PUBLICATION:

How to Parent Your Teenager

To do this job right demands a revolution in your mind and actions. The ways you parented when your child was small no longer apply. Now you need to respond and act in more thoughtful, calm and careful ways.

In this exciting and insightful book, Dale leads you through the conversion you must go through to handle the issues and energies of your teen. He describes in detail how to talk with your teenager and tells you exactly what to say and how to say it.

Filled with dialogues between parents and teens, this book is necessary reading to help you and your teenager enjoy these vital years.

JODA Communications, Ltd.
10125 West North Avenue
Milwaukee, WI 53226
Telephone: 414-475-1600

The next three pages contain ordering information

The Life Skills Series by Dale R. Olen, Ph.D.

Quantity	Title	Unit Price	Total
	Accepting Yourself: Liking Yourself All of the Time (005-9)	$5.95	
	Thinking Reasonably: Reaching Emotional Peace Through Mental Toughness (004-0)	$5.95	
	Meeting Life Head On: Moving into Life with Courage—Not Backing Away in Fear (006-7)	$5.95	
	Managing Stress: Learning to Pace Your Chase Through Life (003-2)	$5.95	
	Communicating: Speaking and Listening to End Misunderstanding and Promote Friendship (007-5)	$5.95	
	Being Intimate: Achieving Union With Others Without Losing Yourself (008-3)	$5.95	
	Reducing Anger: Harnessing Passion and Fury to Work for You—Not Against Others (009-1)	$5.95	
	Overcoming Fear: Reaching for Your Dreams and Knowing Peace of Mind (010-5)	$5.95	
	Defeating Depression: Lifting Yourself from Sadness into Joy (011-3)	$5.95	
	Resolving Conflict: Learning How You Both Can Win and Keep Your Relationship (012-1)	$5.95	
	10-book set of above titles	$49.95	

TOTAL ORDER

Shipping and handling: For 1-2 books, add $1.50; for 3-6 books, add $3.50; for 7-10 books, add $4.50

If Wisconsin resident, add 5% or 5 1/2% sales tax

TOTAL $

METHOD of PAYMENT

☐ Check enclosed. (Make checks payable to JODA Communications, Ltd.)

☐ VISA   ☐ MASTERCARD

Credit Card No. _____ Expiration Date _____

Signature _____

Mail order form along with payment to: **JODA Communications, Ltd.**
10125 West North Avenue, Milwaukee WI 53226

Or you may call **1-414-475-1600.** Please have your VISA or MASTERCARD information ready.

Please send books to:

_____
Name

_____
Street Address

_____
City   State   Zip Code

_____
Phone

ORDER FORM

THE THOUGHTFUL ART OF DISCIPLINE

TEACHING RESPONSIBILITY WHEN YOUR CHILD MISBEHAVES

QUANTITY	No. of COPIES	DISCOUNT	UNIT PRICE	TOTAL
	1-2		8.95	
	3-5	10%	8.06	
	6-10	15%	7.61	
	11-20	20%	7.16	
	over 20	25%	6.71	

Add shipping & handling: 1-2 books, $2.00;
3-5 books, $4.00; 6-10 books, $5.00.
For larger quantities, please call JODA for shipping costs

Wisconsin residents add 5$\frac{1}{2}$% sales tax

TOTAL

METHOD of PAYMENT

❑ **Check enclosed. (Make payable to JODA Communications, Ltd.)**

❑ **VISA**   ❑ **MASTERCARD**

Credit Card No._____Expires_____

Signature_____

Please mail this order form with your payment to:

JODA Communications, Ltd.
10125 West North Avenue, Milwaukee, WI 53226

Or you may call **1-414-475-1600. Please have your VISA or MASTERCARD**
information ready.

Send books to: (PLEASE PRINT)

name
street address
city   state   zip code
phone

ORDER FORM

PARENTING FOR THE FIRST TIME

GETTING OFF TO A HEALTHY START

QUANTITY	No. of COPIES	DISCOUNT	UNIT PRICE	TOTAL
	1-2		8.95	
	3-5	10%	8.06	
	6-10	15%	7.61	
	11-20	20%	7.16	
	over 20	25%	6.71	

Add shipping & handling: 1-2 books, $2.00;
3-5 books, $4.00; 6-10 books, $5.00.
For larger quantities, please call JODA for shipping costs

Wisconsin residents add $5\frac{1}{2}$% sales tax

TOTAL

METHOD of PAYMENT

☐ **Check enclosed. (Make payable to JODA Communications, Ltd.)**

☐ **VISA**   ☐ **MASTERCARD**

Credit Card No._____Expires_____

Signature_____

Please mail this order form with your payment to:

JODA Communications, Ltd.
10125 West North Avenue, Milwaukee, WI 53226

Or you may call **1-414-475-1600.** Please have your **VISA** or **MASTERCARD** information ready.

Send books to:

name
street address
city   state   zip code
phone

THE KYBALION

A STUDY OF

THE HERMETIC PHILOSOPHY

OF ANCIENT EGYPT AND GREECE

By THREE INITIATES

"THE LIPS OF WISDOM ARE CLOSED,
EXCEPT TO THE EARS OF UNDERSTANDING."

The Kybalion
By Three Initiates

Print ISBN 13: 978-1-4209-6119-5
eBook ISBN 13: 978-1-4209-6062-4

Cover Image: a detail of "A Philosopher, possibly Hermes Trismegistus", from Histoire des Philosophes, late 15th century (vellum), French School, (15th century) / Private Collection / Bridgeman Images.

Please visit *www.digireads.com*

CONTENTS

To

HERMES TRISMEGISTUS

KNOWN BY THE ANCIENT EGYPTIANS AS

"THE GREAT GREAT"

AND

"MASTER OF MASTERS"

THIS LITTLE VOLUME OF HERMETIC TEACHINGS
IS REVERENTLY DEDICATED

Introduction

We take great pleasure in presenting to the attention of students and investigator of the Secret Doctrines this little work based upon the world-old Hermetic Teachings. There has been so little written upon this subject, not withstanding the countless references to the Teachings in the many works upon occultism, that the many earnest searchers after the Arcane Truths will doubtless welcome the appearance of this present volume. The purpose of this work is not the enunciation of any special philosophy or doctrine, but rather is to give to the students a statement of the Truth that will serve to reconcile the many bits of occult knowledge that they may have acquired, but which are apparently opposed to each other and which often serve to discourage and disgust the beginner in the study. Our intent is not to erect a new Temple of Knowledge, but rather to place in the hands of the student a Master-Key with which he may open the many inner doors in the Temple of Mystery through the main portals he has already entered.

There is no portion of the occult teachings possessed by the world which have been so closely guarded as the fragments of the Hermetic Teachings which have come down to us over the tens of centuries which have elapsed since the lifetime of its great founder, Hermes Trismegistus, the "scribe of the gods," who dwelt in old Egypt in the days when the present race of men was in its infancy. Contemporary with Abraham, and, if the legends be true, an instructor of that venerable sage, Hermes was, and is, the Great Central Sun of Occultism, whose rays have served to illumine the countless teachings which have been promulgated since his time. All the fundamental and basic teachings embedded in the esoteric teachings of every race may be traced back to Hermes. Even the most ancient teachings of India undoubtedly have their roots in the original Hermetic Teachings.

From the land of the Ganges many advanced occultists wandered to the land of Egypt, and sat at the feet of the Master. From him they obtained the Master-Key which explained and reconciled their divergent views, and thus the Secret Doctrine was firmly established. From other lands also came the learned ones, all of whom regarded Hermes as the Master of Masters, and his influence was so great that in spite of the many wanderings from the path on the part of the centuries of teachers in these different lands, there may still be found a certain basic resemblance and correspondence which underlies the many and often quite divergent theories entertained and taught by the occultists of these different lands today. The student of Comparative Religions will be able to perceive the influence of the Hermetic Teachings in every religion worthy of the name, now known to man, whether it be a dead religion or one in full vigor in our own times. There is always certain

correspondence in spite of the contradictory features, and the Hermetic Teachings act as the Great Reconciler.

The lifework of Hermes seems to have been in the direction of planting the great Seed-Truth which has grown and blossomed in so many strange forms, rather than to establish a school of philosophy which would dominate, the world's thought. But, nevertheless, the original truths taught by him have been kept intact in their original purity by a few men each age, who, refusing great numbers of half-developed students and followers, followed the Hermetic custom and reserved their truth for the few who were ready to comprehend and master it. From lip to ear the truth has been handed down among the few. There have always been a few Initiates in each generation, in the various lands of the earth, who kept alive the sacred flame of the Hermetic Teachings, and such have always been willing to use their lamps to re-light the lesser lamps of the outside world, when the light of truth grew dim, and clouded by reason of neglect, and when the wicks became clogged with foreign matter. There were always a few to tend faithfully the altar of the Truth, upon which was kept alight the Perpetual Lamp of Wisdom. These men devoted their lives to the labor of love which the poet has so well stated in his lines:

"O, let not the flame die out! Cherished age after age in its dark cavern—in its holy temples cherished. Fed by pure ministers of love— let not the flame die out!"

These men have never sought popular approval, nor numbers of followers. They are indifferent to these things, for they know how few there are in each generation who are ready for the truth, or who would recognize it if it were presented to them. They reserve the "strong meat for men," while others furnish the "milk for babes." They reserve their pearls of wisdom for the few elect, who recognize their value and who wear them in their crowns, instead of casting them before the materialistic vulgar swine, who would trample them in the mud and mix them with their disgusting mental food. But still these men have never forgotten or overlooked the original teachings of Hermes, regarding the passing on of the words of truth to those ready to receive it, which teaching is stated in The Kybalion as follows: "Where fall the footsteps of the Master, the ears of those ready for his Teaching open wide." And again: "When the ears of the student are ready to hear, then cometh the lips to fill them with wisdom." But their customary attitude has always been strictly in accordance with the other Hermetic aphorism, also in The Kybalion: "The lips of Wisdom are closed, except to the ears of Understanding."

There are those who have criticized this attitude of the Hermetists, and who have claimed that they did not manifest the proper spirit in their policy of seclusion and reticence. But a moment's glance back: over the pages of history will show the wisdom of the Masters, who

knew the folly of attempting to teach to the world that which it was neither ready or willing to receive. The Hermetists have never sought to be martyrs, and have, instead, sat silently aside with a pitying smile on their closed lips, while the "heathen raged noisily about them" in their customary amusement of putting to death and torture the honest but misguided enthusiasts who imagined that they could force upon a race of barbarians the truth capable of being understood only by the elect who had advanced along The Path. And the spirit of persecution has not as yet died out in the land. There are certain Hermetic Teachings, which, if publicly promulgated, would bring down upon the teachers a great cry of scorn and revilement from the multitude, who would again raise the cry of "Crucify! Crucify." In this little work we have endeavored to give you an idea of the fundamental teachings of The Kybalion, striving to give you the working Principles, leaving you to apply them yourselves, rather than attempting to work out the teaching in detail. If you are a true student, you will be able to work out and apply these Principles—if not, then you must develop yourself into one, for otherwise the Hermetic Teachings will be as "words, words, words" to you.

THE THREE INITIATES.

Chapter I. The Hermetic Philosophy

"The lips of wisdom are closed, except to the ears of Understanding"—*The Kybalion.*

From old Egypt have come the fundamental esoteric and occult teachings which have so strongly influenced the philosophies of all races, nations and peoples, for several thousand years. Egypt, the home of the Pyramids and the Sphinx, was the birthplace of the Hidden Wisdom and Mystic Teachings. From her Secret Doctrine all nations have borrowed. India, Persia, Chaldea, Medea, China, Japan, Assyria, ancient Greece and Rome, and other ancient countries partook liberally at the feast of knowledge which the Hierophants and Masters of the Land of Isis so freely provided for those who came prepared to partake of the great store of Mystic and Occult Lore which the masterminds of that ancient land had gathered together.

In ancient Egypt dwelt the great Adepts and Masters who have never been surpassed, and who seldom have been equaled, during the centuries that have taken their processional flight since the days of the Great Hermes. In Egypt was located the Great Lodge of Lodges of the Mystics. At the doors of her Temples entered the Neophytes who afterward, as Hierophants, Adepts, and Masters, traveled to the four corners of the earth, carrying with them the precious knowledge which they were ready, anxious, and willing to pass on to those who were ready to receive the same. All students of the Occult recognize the debt that they owe to these venerable Masters of that ancient land.

But among these great Masters of Ancient Egypt there once dwelt one of whom Masters hailed as "The Master of Masters." This man, if "man" indeed he was, dwelt in Egypt in the earliest days. He was known as Hermes Trismegistus. He was the father of the Occult Wisdom; the founder of Astrology; the discoverer of Alchemy. The details of his life story are lost to history, owing to the lapse of the years, though several of the ancient countries disputed with each other in their claims to the honor of having furnished his birthplace—and this thousands of years ago. The date of his sojourn in Egypt, in that his last incarnation on this planet, is not now known, but it has been fixed at the early days of the oldest dynasties of Egypt—long before the days of Moses. The best authorities regard him as a contemporary of Abraham, and some of the Jewish traditions go so far as to claim that Abraham acquired a portion of his mystic knowledge from Hermes himself.

As the years rolled by after his passing from this plane of life (tradition recording that he lived three hundred years in the flesh), the Egyptians deified Hermes, and made him one of their gods, under the name of Thoth. Years after, the people of Ancient Greece also made

him one of their many gods—calling him "Hermes, the god of Wisdom." The Egyptians revered his memory for many centuries—yes, tens of centuries—calling him "the Scribe of the Gods," and bestowing upon him, distinctively, his ancient title, "Trismegistus," which means "the thrice-great"; "the great-great"; "the greatest-great"; etc. In all the ancient lands, the name of Hermes Trismegistus was revered, the name being synonymous with the "Fount of Wisdom."

Even to this day, we use the term "hermetic" in the sense of "secret"; "sealed so that nothing can escape"; etc., and this by reason of the fact that the followers of Hermes always observed the principle of secrecy in their teachings. They did not believe in "casting pearls before swine," but rather held to the teaching "milk for babes"; "meat for strong men," both of which maxims are familiar to readers of the Christian scriptures, but both of which had been used by the Egyptians for centuries before the Christian era.

And this policy of careful dissemination of the truth has always characterized the Hermetics, even unto the present day. The Hermetic Teachings are to be found in all lands, among all religions, but never identified with any particular country, nor with any particular religious sect. This because of the warning of the ancient teachers against allowing the Secret Doctrine to become crystallized into a creed. The wisdom of this caution is apparent to all students of history. The ancient occultism of India and Persia degenerated, and was largely lost, owing to the fact that the teachers became priests, and so mixed theology with the philosophy, the result being that the occultism of India and Persia has been gradually lost amidst the mass of religious superstition, cults, creeds and "gods." So it was with Ancient Greece and Rome. So it was with the Hermetic Teachings of the Gnostics and Early Christians, which were lost at the time of Constantine, whose iron hand smothered philosophy with the blanket of theology, losing to the Christian Church that which was its very essence and spirit, and causing it to grope throughout several centuries before it found the way back to its ancient faith, the indications apparent to all careful observers in this Twentieth Century being that the Church is now struggling to get back to its ancient mystic teachings. But there were always a few faithful souls who kept alive the Flame, tending it carefully, and not allowing its light to become extinguished. And thanks to these staunch hearts, and fearless minds, we have the truth still with us.

But it is not found in books, to any great extent. It has been passed along from Master to Student; from Initiate to Hierophant; from lip to ear. When it was written down at all, its meaning was veiled in terms of alchemy and astrology so that only those possessing the key could read it aright. This was made necessary in order to avoid the persecutions of the theologians of the Middle Ages, who fought the Secret Doctrine with fire and sword; stake, gibbet and cross. Even to this day there will

be found but few reliable books on the Hermetic Philosophy, although there are countless references to it in many books written on various phases of Occultism. And yet, the Hermetic Philosophy is the only Master Key which will open all the doors of the Occult Teachings!

In the early days, there was a compilation of certain Basic Hermetic Doctrines, passed on from teacher to student, which was known as "THE KYBALION," the exact significance and meaning of the term having been lost for several centuries. This teaching, however, is known to many to whom it has descended, from mouth to ear, on and on throughout the centuries. Its precepts have never been written down, or printed, so far as we know. It was merely a collection of maxims, axioms, and precepts, which were non-understandable to outsiders, but which were readily understood by students, after the axioms, maxims, and precepts had been explained and exemplified by the Hermetic Initiates to their Neophytes. These teachings really constituted the basic principles of "The Art of Hermetic Alchemy," which, contrary to the general belief, dealt in the mastery of Mental Forces, rather than Material Elements—the Transmutation of one kind of Mental Vibrations into others, instead of the changing of one kind of metal into another. The legends of the "Philosopher's Stone" which would turn base metal into Gold, was an allegory relating to Hermetic Philosophy, readily understood by all students of true Hermeticism.

In this little book, of which this is the First Lesson, we invite our students to examine into the Hermetic Teachings, as set forth in THE KYBALION, and as explained by ourselves, humble students of the Teachings, who, while bearing the title of Initiates, are still students at the feet of HERMES, the Master. We herein give you many of the maxims, axioms and precepts of THE KYBALION accompanied by explanations and illustrations which we deem likely to render the teachings more easily comprehended by the modern student, particularly as the original text is purposely veiled in obscure terms.

The original maxims, axioms, and precepts of THE KYBALION are printed herein, in italics, the proper credit being given. Our own work is printed in the regular way, in the body of the work. We trust that the many students to whom we now offer this little work will derive as much benefit from the study of its pages as have the many who have gone on before, treading the same Path to Mastery throughout the centuries that have passed since the times of HERMES TRISMEGISTUS—the Master of Masters—the Great-Great. In the words of "THE KYBALION":

"Where fall the footsteps of the Master, the ears of those ready for his Teaching open wide."—*The Kybalion.*

"When the ears of the student are ready to hear, then cometh the lips to fill them with Wisdom."—*The Kybalion.*

So that according to the Teachings, the passage of this book to those ready for the instruction will attract the attention of such as are prepared to receive the Teaching. And, likewise, when the pupil is ready to receive the truth, then will this little book come to him, or her. Such is The Law. The Hermetic Principle of Cause and Effect, in its aspect of The Law of Attraction, will bring lips and ear together—pupil and book in company. So mote it be!

Chapter II. *The Seven Hermetic Principles*

"The Principles of Truth are Seven; he who knows these, understandingly, possesses the Magic Key before whose touch all the Doors of the Temple fly open."—*The Kybalion.*

The Seven Hermetic Principles, upon which the entire Hermetic Philosophy is based, are as follows:

THE PRINCIPLE OF MENTALISM.
THE PRINCIPLE OF CORRESPONDENCE.
THE PRINCIPLE OF VIBRATION.
THE PRINCIPLE OF POLARITY.
THE PRINCIPLE OF RHYTHM.
THE PRINCIPLE OF CAUSE AND EFFECT.
THE PRINCIPLE OF GENDER.

These Seven Principles will be discussed and explained as we proceed with these lessons. A short explanation of each, however, may as well be given at this point.

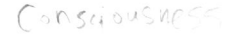

I. THE PRINCIPLE OF MENTALISM

"THE ALL IS MIND; The Universe is Mental."—*The Kybalion.*

This Principle embodies the truth that "All is Mind." It explains that THE ALL (which is the Substantial Reality underlying all the outward manifestations and appearances which we know under the terms of "The Material Universe"; the "Phenomena of Life"; "Matter"; "Energy"; and, in short, all that is apparent to our material senses) is SPIRIT which in itself is UNKNOWABLE and UNDEFINABLE, but which may be considered and thought of as AN UNIVERSAL, INFINITE, LIVING MIND. It also explains that all the phenomenal world or universe is simply a Mental Creation of THE ALL, subject to the Laws of Created Things, and that the universe, as a whole, and in its parts or units, has its existence in the Mind of THE ALL, in which Mind we "live and move and have our being." This Principle, by establishing the Mental Nature of the Universe, easily explains all of the varied mental and psychic phenomena that occupy such a large portion of the public attention, and which, without such explanation, are non-understandable and defy scientific treatment. An understanding of this great Hermetic Principle of Mentalism enables the individual to readily grasp the laws of the Mental Universe, and to apply the same to his well-being and advancement. The Hermetic Student is enabled to

apply intelligently the great Mental Laws, instead of using them in a haphazard manner. With the Master-Key in his possession, the student may unlock the many doors of the mental and psychic temple of knowledge, and enter the same freely and intelligently. This Principle explains the true nature of "Energy," "Power," and "Matter," and why and how all these are subordinate to the Mastery of Mind. One of the old Hermetic Masters wrote, long ages ago: "He who grasps the truth of the Mental Nature of the Universe is well advanced on The Path to Mastery." And these words are as true today as at the time they were first written. Without this Master-Key, Mastery is impossible, and the student knocks in vain at the many doors of The Temple.

II. THE PRINCIPLE OF CORRESPONDENCE

"As above, so below; as below, so above."—*The Kybalion.*

This Principle embodies the truth that there is always a Correspondence between the laws and phenomena of the various planes of Being and Life. The old Hermetic axiom ran in these words: "As above, so below; as below, so above." and the grasping of this Principle gives one the means of solving many a dark paradox, and hidden secret of Nature. There are planes beyond our knowing, but when we apply the Principle of Correspondence to them we are able to understand much that would otherwise be unknowable to us. This Principle is of universal application and manifestation, on the various planes of the material, mental, and spiritual universe—it is an Universal Law. The ancient Hermetists considered this Principle as one of the most important mental instruments by which man was able to pry aside the obstacles which hid from view the Unknown. Its use even tore aside the Veil of Isis to the extent that a glimpse of the face of the goddess might be caught. Just as a knowledge of the Principles of Geometry enables man to measure distant suns and their movements, while seated in his observatory, so a knowledge of the Principle of Correspondence enables Man to reason intelligently from the Known to the Unknown. Studying the monad, he understands the archangel.

III. THE PRINCIPLE OF VIBRATION

"Nothing rests; everything moves; everything vibrates."—*The Kybalion.*

This Principle embodies the truth that "everything is in motion"; "everything vibrates"; "nothing is at rest"; facts which Modern Science endorses, and which each new scientific discovery tends to verify. And yet this Hermetic Principle was enunciated thousands of years ago, by

the Masters of Ancient Egypt. This Principle explains that the differences between different manifestations of Matter, Energy, Mind, and even Spirit, result largely from varying rates of Vibration. From THE ALL, which is Pure Spirit, down to the grossest form of Matter, all is in vibration—the higher the vibration, the higher the position in the scale. The vibration of Spirit is at such an infinite rate of intensity and rapidity that it is practically at rest—just as a rapidly moving wheel seems to be motionless. And at the other end of the scale, there are gross forms of matter whose vibrations are so low as to seem at rest. Between these poles, there are millions upon millions of varying degrees of vibration. From corpuscle and electron, atom and molecule, to worlds and universes, everything is in vibratory motion. This is also true on the planes of energy and force (which are but varying degrees of vibration); and also on the mental planes (whose states depend upon vibrations); and even on to the spiritual planes. An understanding of this Principle, with the appropriate formulas, enables Hermetic students to control their own mental vibrations as well as those of others. The Masters also apply this Principle to the conquering of Natural phenomena, in various ways. "He who understands the Principle of Vibration, has grasped the sceptre of power," says one of the old writers.

IV. THE PRINCIPLE OF POLARITY

"Everything is Dual; everything has poles; everything has its pair of opposites; like and unlike are the same; opposites are identical in nature, but different in degree; extremes meet; all truths are but half-truths; all paradoxes may be reconciled."—*The Kybalion.*

This Principle embodies the truth that "everything is dual"; "everything has two poles"; "everything has its pair of opposites," all of which were old Hermetic axioms. It explains the old paradoxes, that have perplexed so many, which have been stated as follows: "Thesis and antithesis are identical in nature, but different in degree"; "opposites are the same, differing only in degree"; "the pairs of opposites may be reconciled"; "extremes meet"; "everything is and isn't, at the same time"; "all truths are but half truths"; "every truth is half-false"; "there are two sides to everything," etc., etc., etc. It explains that in everything there are two poles, or opposite aspects, and that "opposites" are really only the two extremes of the same thing, with many varying degrees between them. To illustrate: Heat and Cold, although "opposites," are really the same thing, the differences consisting merely of degrees of the same thing. Look at your thermometer and see if you can discover where "heat" terminates and "cold" begins! There is no such thing as "absolute heat" or "absolute

cold"—the two terms "heat" and "cold" simply indicate varying degrees of the same thing, and that "same thing" which manifests as "heat" and "cold" is merely a form, variety, and rate of Vibration. So "heat" and "cold" are simply the "two poles" of that which we call "Heat"—and the phenomena attendant thereupon are manifestations of the Principle of Polarity. The same Principle manifests in the case of "Light and Darkness," which are the same thing, the difference consisting of varying degrees between the two poles of the phenomena. Where does "darkness" leave off, and "light" begin? What is the difference between "Large and Small"? Between "Hard and Soft"? Between "Black and White"? Between "Sharp and Dull"? Between "Noise and Quiet"? Between "High and Low"? Between "Positive and Negative"? The Principle of Polarity explains these paradoxes, and no other Principle can supersede it. The same Principle operates on the Mental Plane. Let us take a radical and extreme example—that of "Love and Hate," two mental states apparently totally different. And yet there are degrees of Hate and degrees of Love, and a middle point in which we use the terms "Like or Dislike," which shade into each other so gradually that sometimes we are at a loss to know whether we "like" or "dislike" or "neither." And all are simply degrees of the same thing, as you will see if you will but think a moment. And, more than this (and considered of more importance by the Hermetists), it is possible to change the vibrations of Hate to the vibrations of Love, in one's own mind, and in the minds of others. Many of you, who read these lines, have had personal experiences of the involuntary rapid transition from Love to Hate, and the reverse, in your own case and that of others. And you will therefore realize the possibility of this being accomplished by the use of the Will, by means of the Hermetic formulas. "Good and Evil" are but the poles of the same thing, and the Hermetist understands the art of transmuting Evil into Good, by means of an application of the Principle of Polarity. In short, the "Art of Polarization becomes a phase of "Mental Alchemy" known and practiced by the ancient and modern Hermetic Masters. An understanding of the Principle will enable one to change his own Polarity, as well as that of others, if he will devote the time and study necessary to master the art.

V. THE PRINCIPLE OF RHYTHM

"Everything flows, out and in; everything has its tides; all things rise and fall; the pendulum-swing manifests in everything; the measure of the swing to the right is the measure of the swing to the left; rhythm compensates."—*The Kybalion*

This Principle embodies the truth that in everything there is manifested a measured motion, to and fro; a flow and inflow; a swing backward and forward; a pendulum-like movement; a tide-like ebb and flow; a high-tide and low-tide; between the two poles which exist in accordance with the Principle of Polarity described a moment ago. There is always an action and a reaction; an advance and a retreat; a rising and a sinking. This is in the affairs of the Universe, suns, worlds, men, animals, mind, energy, and matter. This law is manifest in the creation and destruction of worlds; in the rise and fall of nations; in the life of all things; and finally in the mental states of Man (and it is with this latter that the Hermetists find the understanding of the Principle most important). The Hermetists have grasped this Principle, finding its universal application, and have also discovered certain means to overcome its effects in themselves by the use of the appropriate formulas and methods. They apply the Mental Law of Neutralization. They cannot annul the Principle, or cause it to cease its operation, but they have learned how to escape its effects upon themselves to a certain degree depending upon the Mastery of the Principle. They have learned how to USE it, instead of being USED BY it. In this and similar methods, consist the Art of the Hermetists. The Master of Hermetics polarizes himself at the point at which he desires to rest, and then neutralizes the Rhythmic swing of the pendulum which would tend to carry him to the other pole. All individuals who have attained any degree of Self-Mastery do this to a certain degree, more or less unconsciously, but the Master does this consciously, and by the use of his Will, and attains a degree of Poise and Mental Firmness almost impossible of belief on the part of the masses who are swung backward and forward like a pendulum. This Principle and that of Polarity have been closely studied by the Hermetists, and the methods of counteracting, neutralizing, and USING them form an important part of the Hermetic Mental Alchemy.

VI. THE PRINCIPLE OF CAUSE AND EFFECT

"Every Cause has its Effect; every Effect has its Cause; everything happens according to Law; Chance is but a name for Law not recognized; there are many planes of causation, but nothing escapes the Law."—*The Kybalion*

This Principle embodies the fact that there is a Cause for every Effect; an Effect from every Cause. It explains that: "Everything Happens according to Law"; that nothing ever "merely happens"; that there is no such thing as Chance; that while there are various planes of Cause and Effect, the higher dominating—the lower planes, still

nothing ever entirely escapes the Law. The Hermetists understand the art and methods of rising above the ordinary plane of Cause and Effect, to a certain degree, and by mentally rising to a higher plane they become Causers instead of Effects. The masses of people are carried along, obedient to environment; the wills and desires of others stronger than themselves; heredity; suggestion; and other outward causes moving them about like pawns on the Chessboard of Life. But the Masters, rising to the plane above, dominate their moods, characters, qualities, and powers, as well as the environment surrounding them, and become Movers instead of pawns. They help to PLAY THE GAME OF LIFE, instead of being played and moved about by other wills and environment. They USE the Principle instead of being its tools. The Masters obey the Causation of the higher planes, but they help to RULE on their own plane. In this statement there is condensed a wealth of Hermetic knowledge—let him read who can.

VII. THE PRINCIPLE OF GENDER

"Gender is in everything; everything has its Masculine and Feminine Principles; Gender manifests on all planes."—*The Kybalion*

This Principle embodies the truth that there is GENDER manifested in everything—the Masculine and Feminine Principles ever at work. This is true not only of the Physical Plane, but of the Mental and even the Spiritual Planes. On the Physical Plane, the Principle manifests as SEX, on the higher planes it takes higher forms, but the Principle is ever the same. No creation, physical, mental or spiritual, is possible without this Principle. An understanding of its laws will throw light on many a subject that has perplexed the minds of men. The Principle of Gender works ever in the direction of generation, regeneration, and creation. Everything, and every person, contains the two Elements or Principles, or this great Principle, within it, him or her. Every Male thing has the Female Element also; every Female contains also the Male Principle. If you would understand the philosophy of Mental and Spiritual Creation, Generation, and Re-generation, you must understand and study this Hermetic Principle. It contains the solution of many mysteries of Life. We caution you that this Principle has no reference to the many base, pernicious and degrading lustful theories, teachings and practices, which are taught under fanciful titles, and which are a prostitution of the great natural principle of Gender. Such base revivals of the ancient infamous forms of Phallicism tend to ruin mind, body and soul, and the Hermetic Philosophy has ever sounded the warning note against these degraded teachings which tend toward lust, licentiousness, and perversion of Nature's principles. If you seek such teachings, you must go elsewhere for them—

Hermeticism contains nothing for you along these lines. To the pure, all things are pure; to the base, all things are base.

Chapter III. *Mental Transmutation*

"Mind (as well as metals and elements) may be transmuted, from state to state; degree to degree; condition to condition; pole to pole; vibration to vibration. True Hermetic Transmutation is a Mental Art."—
The Kybalion.

As we have stated, the Hermetists were the original alchemists, astrologers, and psychologists, Hermes having been the founder of these schools of thought. From astrology has grown modern astronomy; from alchemy has grown modern chemistry; from the mystic psychology has grown the modern psychology of the schools. But it must not be supposed that the ancients were ignorant of that which the modern schools suppose to be their exclusive and special property. The records engraved on the stones of Ancient Egypt show conclusively that the ancients had a full comprehensive knowledge of astronomy, the very building of the Pyramids showing the connection between their design and the study of astronomical science. Nor were they ignorant of Chemistry, for the fragments of the ancient writings show that they were acquainted with the chemical properties of things; in fact, the ancient theories regarding physics are being slowly verified by the latest discoveries of modern science, notably those relating to the constitution of matter. Nor must it be supposed that they were ignorant of the so-called modern discoveries in psychology—on the contrary, the Egyptians were especially skilled in the science of Psychology, particularly in the branches that the modern schools ignore, but which, nevertheless, are being uncovered under the name of "psychic science" which is perplexing the psychologists of to-day, and making them reluctantly admit that "there may be something in it after all."

The truth is, that beneath the material chemistry, astronomy and psychology (that is, the psychology in its phase of "brain action") the ancients possessed a knowledge of transcendental astronomy, called astrology; of transcendental chemistry, called alchemy; of transcendental psychology, called mystic psychology. They possessed the Inner Knowledge as well as the Outer Knowledge, the latter alone being possessed by modern scientists. Among the many secret branches of knowledge possessed by the Hermetists, was that Transmutation, which known as Mental forms the subject matter of this lesson.

"Transmutation" is a term usually employed to designate the ancient art of the transmutation of metals—particularly of the base metals into gold. The word "Transmute" means "to change from one nature, form, or substance, into another to transform" (Webster). And accordingly, "Mental Transmutation" means the art of changing and transforming mental states, forms, and conditions, into others. So you

may see that Mental Transmutation is the "Art of Mental Chemistry," if you like the term—a form of practical Mystic Psychology.

But this means far more than appears on the surface. Transmutation, Alchemy, or Chemistry on the Mental Plane is important enough in its effects, to be sure, and if the art stopped there it would still be one of the most important branches of study known to man. But this is only the beginning. Let us see why!

The first of the Seven Hermetic Principles is the Principle of Mentalism, the axiom of which is "THE ALL is Mind; the Universe is Mental," which means that the Underlying Reality of the Universe is Mind; and the Universe itself is Mental—that is, "existing in the Mind of THE ALL." We shall consider this Principle in succeeding lessons, but let us see the effect of the principle if it be assumed to be true.

If the Universal is Mental in its nature, then Mental Transmutation must be the art of CHANGING THE CONDITIONS OF THE UNIVERSE, along the lines of Matter, Force and mind. So you see, therefore, that Mental Transmutation is really the "Magic" of which the ancient; writers had so much to say in their mystical works, and about which they gave so few practical instructions. If All be Mental, then the art which enables one to transmute mental conditions must render the Master the controller of material conditions as well as those ordinarily called "mental."

As a matter of fact, none but advanced Mental Alchemists have been able to attain the degree of power necessary to control the grosser physical conditions, such as the control of the elements of Nature; the production or cessation of tempests; the production and cessation of earthquakes and other great physical phenomena. But that such men have existed, and do exist today, is a matter of earnest belief to all advanced occultists of all schools. That the Masters exist, and have these powers, the best teachers assure their students, having had experiences which justify them in such belief and statements. These Masters do not make public exhibitions of their powers, but seek seclusion from the crowds of men, in order to better work their may along the Path of Attainment. We mention their existence, at this point, merely to call your attention to the fact that their power is entirely Mental, and operates along the lines of the higher Mental Transmutation, under the Hermetic Principle of Mentalism. "The Universe is Mental"—The Kybalion.

But students and Hermetists of lesser degree than Masters—the Initiates and Teachers—are able to freely work along the Mental Plane, in Mental Transmutation. In fact all that we call "psychic phenomena,"; "mental influence"; "mental science"; "new-thought phenomena," etc., operates along the same general lines, for there is but one principle involved, no matter by what name the phenomena be called.

The student and practitioner of Mental Transmutation works

among the Mental Plane, transmuting mental conditions, states, etc., into others, according to various formulas, more or less efficacious. The various "treatments," "affirmations," "denials" etc., of the schools of mental science are but formulas, often quite imperfect and unscientific, of The Hermetic Art. The majority of modern practitioners are quite ignorant compared to the ancient masters, for they lack the fundamental knowledge upon which the work is based.

Not only may the mental states, etc., of one's self be changed or transmuted by Hermetic Methods; but also the states of others may be, and are, constantly transmuted in the same way, usually unconsciously, but often consciously by some understanding the laws and principles, in cases where the people affected are not informed of the principles of self-protection. And more than this, as many students and practitioners of modern mental science know, every material condition depending upon the minds of other people may be changed or transmuted in accordance with the earnest desire, will, and "treatments" of person desiring changed conditions of life. The public are so generally informed regarding these things at present, that we do not deem it necessary to mention the same at length, our purpose at this point being merely to show the Hermetic Principle and Art underlying all of these various forms of practice, good and evil, for the force can be used in opposite directions according to the Hermetic Principles of Polarity.

In this little book we shall state the basic principles of Mental Transmutation, that all who read may grasp the Underlying Principles, and thus possess the Master-Key that will unlock the many doors of the Principle of Polarity.

We shall now proceed to a consideration of the first of the Hermetic Seven Principles—the Principle of Mentalism, in which is explained the truth that "THE ALL is Mind; the Universe is Mental," in the words of The Kybalion. We ask the close attention, and careful study of this great Principle, on the part of our students, for it is really the Basic Principle of the whole Hermetic Philosophy, and of the Hermetic Art of Mental Transmutation.

Chapter IV. The All

"Under, and back of, the Universe of Time, Space and Change, is ever to be found The Substantial Reality—the Fundamental Truth."— *The Kybalion.*

"Substance" means: "that which underlies all outward manifestations; the essence; the essential reality; the thing in itself," etc. "Substantial" means: "actually existing; being the essential element; being real," etc. "Reality" means:" the state of being real; true, enduring; valid; fixed; permanent; actual," etc.

Under and behind all outward appearances or manifestations, there must always be a Substantial Reality. This is the Law. Man considering the Universe, of which he is a unit, sees nothing but change in matter, forces, and mental states. He sees that nothing really IS, but that everything is BECOMING and CHANGING. Nothing stands still—everything is being born, growing, dying—the very instant a thing reaches its height, it begins to decline—the law of rhythm is in constant operation—there is no reality, enduring quality, fixity, or substantiality in anything—nothing is permanent but Change. He sees all things evolving from other things, and resolving into other things—a constant action and reaction; inflow and outflow; building up and tearing down; creation and destruction; birth, growth and death. Nothing endures but Change. And if he be a thinking man, he realizes that all of these changing things must be but outward appearances or manifestations of some Underlying Power—some Substantial Reality.

All thinkers, in all lands and in all times, have assumed the necessity for postulating the existence of this Substantial Reality. All philosophies worthy of the name have been based upon this thought. Men have given to this Substantial Reality many names—some have called it by the term of Deity (under many titles). Others have called it "The Infinite and Eternal Energy" others have tried to call it "Matter"—but all have acknowledged its existence. It is self-evident it needs no argument.

In these lessons we have followed the example of some of the world's greatest thinkers, both ancient and modern—the Hermetic. Masters—and have called this Underlying Power—this Substantial Reality—by the Hermetic name of "THE ALL," which term we consider the most comprehensive of the many terms applied by Man to THAT which transcends names and terms.

We accept and teach the view of the great Hermetic thinkers of all times, as well as of those illumined souls who have reached higher planes of being, both of whom assert that the inner nature of THE ALL is UNKNOWABLE. This must be so, for naught by THE ALL itself

can comprehend its own nature and being.

The Hermetists believe and teach that THE ALL, "in itself," is and must ever be UNKNOWABLE. They regard all the theories, guesses and speculations of the theologians and metaphysicians regarding the inner nature of THE ALL, as but the childish efforts of mortal minds to grasp the secret of the Infinite. Such efforts have always failed and will always fail, from the very nature of the task. One pursuing such inquiries travels around and around in the labyrinth of thought, until he is lost to all sane reasoning, action or conduct, and is utterly unfitted for the work of life. He is like the squirrel which frantically runs around and around the circling treadmill wheel of his cage, traveling ever and yet reaching nowhere—at the end a prisoner still, and standing just where he started.

And still more presumptuous are those who attempt to ascribe to THE ALL the personality, qualities, properties, characteristics and attributes of themselves, ascribing to THE ALL the human emotions, feelings, and characteristics, even down to the pettiest qualities of mankind, such as jealousy, susceptibility to flattery and praise, desire for offerings and worship, and all the other survivals from the days of the childhood of the race. Such ideas are not worthy of grown men and women, and are rapidly being discarded.

(At this point, it may be proper for me to state that we make a distinction between Religion and Theology—between Philosophy and Metaphysics. Religion, to us, means that intuitional realization of the existence of THE ALL, and one's relationship to it; while Theology means the attempts of men to ascribe personality, qualities, and characteristics to it; their theories regarding its affairs, will, desires, plans, and designs, and their assumption of the office of "middle-men" between THE ALL and the people. Philosophy, to us, means the inquiry after knowledge of things knowable and thinkable; while Metaphysical means the attempt to carry the inquiry over and beyond the boundaries and into regions unknowable and unthinkable, and with the same tendency as that of Theology. And consequently, both Religion and Philosophy mean to us things having roots in Reality, while Theology and Metaphysics seem like broken reeds, rooted in the quicksands of ignorance, and affording naught but the most insecure support for the mind or soul of Man. we do not insist upon our students accepting these definitions—we mention them merely to show our position. At any rate, you shall hear very little about Theology and Metaphysics in these lessons.)

But while the essential nature of THE ALL is Unknowable, there are certain truths connected with its existence which the human mind finds itself compelled to accept. And an examination of these reports form a proper subject of inquiry, particularly as they agree with the reports of the Illumined on higher planes. And to this inquiry we now

invite you.

"THAT which is the Fundamental Truth—the Substantial Reality—is beyond true naming, but the Wise Men call it THE ALL."—*The Kybalion.*

"In its Essence, THE ALL is UNKNOWABLE."—*The Kybalion.*

"But, the report of Reason must be hospitably received, and treated with respect."—*The Kybalion.*

The human reason, whose reports we must accept so long as we think at all, informs us as follows regarding THE ALL, and that without attempting to remove the veil of the Unknowable:

(1) THE ALL must be ALL that REALLY IS. There can be nothing existing outside of THE ALL, else THE ALL would not be THE ALL.

(2) THE ALL must be INFINITE, for there is nothing else to define, confine, bound, limit; or restrict THE ALL. It must be Infinite in Time, or ETERNAL,—it must have always continuously existed, for there is nothing else to have ever created it, and something can never evolve from nothing, and if it had ever "not been," even for a moment, it would not "be" now,—it must continuously exist forever, for there is nothing to destroy it, and it can never "not-be," even for a moment, because something can never become nothing. It must be Infinite in Space—it must be Everywhere, for there is no place outside of THE ALL—it cannot be otherwise than continuous in Space, without break, cessation, separation, or interruption, for there is nothing to break, separate, or interrupt its continuity, and nothing with which to "fill in the gaps." It must be Infinite in Power, or Absolute, for there is nothing to limit, restrict, restrain, confine, disturb or condition it—it is subject to no other Power, for there is no other Power.

(3) THE ALL must be IMMUTABLE, or not subject to change in its real nature, for there is nothing to work changes upon it nothing into which it could change, nor from which it could have changed. It cannot be added to nor subtracted from; increased nor diminished; nor become greater or lesser in any respect whatsoever. It must have always been, and must always remain, just what it is now—THE ALL—there has never been, is not now, and never will be, anything else into which it can change.

THE ALL being Infinite, Absolute, Eternal and Unchangeable it must follow that anything finite, changeable, fleeting, and conditioned cannot be THE ALL. And as there is Nothing outside of THE ALL, in Reality, then any and all such finite things must be as Nothing in Reality. Now do not become befogged, nor frightened—we are not trying to lead you into the Christian Science field under cover of Hermetic Philosophy. There is a Reconciliation of this apparently

contradictory state of affairs. Be patient, we will reach it in time.

We see around us that which is called " Matter," which forms the physical foundation for all forms. Is THE ALL merely Matter? Not at all! Matter cannot manifest Life or Mind, and as Life and Mind are manifested in the Universe, THE ALL cannot be Matter, for nothing rises higher than its own source—nothing is ever manifested in an effect that is not in the cause—nothing is evolved as a consequent that is not involved as an antecedent. And then Modern Science informs us that there is really no such thing as Matter—that what we call Matter is merely "interrupted energy or force," that is, energy or force at a low rate of vibration. As a recent writer has said "Matter has melted into Mystery." Even Material Science has abandoned the theory of Matter, and now rests on the basis of "Energy."

Then is THE ALL mere Energy or Force? Not Energy or Force as the materialists use the terms, for their energy and force are blind, mechanical things, devoid of Life or Mind. Life and Mind can never evolve from blind Energy or Force, for the reason given a moment ago: "Nothing can rise higher than its source—nothing is evolved unless it is involved—nothing manifests in the effect, unless it is in the cause." And so THE ALL cannot be mere Energy or Force, for, if it were, then there would be no such things as Life and Mind in existence, and we know better than that, for we are Alive and using Mind to consider this very question, and so are those who claim that Energy or Force is Everything.

What is there then higher than Matter or Energy that we know to be existent in the Universe? LIFE AND MIND! Life and Mind in all their varying degrees of unfoldment! "Then," you ask, "do you mean to tell us that THE ALL is LIFE and MIND?" Yes! and No! is our answer. If you mean Life and Mind as we poor petty mortals know them, we say No! THE ALL is not that! "But what kind of Life and Mind do you mean?" you ask. The answer is "LIVING MIND," as far above that which mortals know by those words, as Life and Mind are higher than mechanical forces, or matter—INFINITE LIVING MIND as compared to finite Life and Mind." We mean that which the illumined souls mean when they reverently pronounce the word: "SPIRIT!" "THE ALL" is Infinite Living Mind the Illumined call it SPIRIT!

Chapter V. The Mental Universe

"The Universe is Mental—held in the Mind of THE ALL."—*The Kybalion.*

THE ALL is SPIRIT! But what is Spirit? This question cannot be answered, for the reason that its definition is practically that of THE ALL, which cannot be explained or defined. Spirit is simply a name that men give to the highest conception of Infinite Living Mind—it means "the Real Essence"—it means Living Mind, as much superior to Life and Mind as we know them, as the latter are superior to mechanical Energy and Matter. Spirit transcends our understanding, and we use the term merely that we may think or speak of THE ALL. For the purposes of thought and understanding, we are justified in thinking of Spirit as Infinite Living Mind, at the same time acknowledging that we cannot fully understand it. We must either do this or stop thinking of the matter at all.

Let us now proceed to a consideration of the nature of the Universe, as a whole and in its parts. What is the Universe? We have seen that there can be nothing outside of THE ALL. Then is the Universe THE ALL? No, this cannot be, because the Universe seems to be made up of MANY and is constantly changing, and in other ways it does not measure up to the ideas that we are compelled to accept regarding THE ALL, as stated in our last lesson. Then if the Universe be not THE ALL, then it must be Nothing—such is the inevitable conclusion of the mind at first thought. But this will not satisfy the question, for we are sensible of the existence of the Universe. Then if the Universe is neither THE ALL, nor Nothing, what Can it be? Let us examine this question.

If the Universe exists at all, or seems to exist, it must proceed in some way from THE ALL—it must be a creation of THE ALL. But as something can never come from nothing, from what could THE ALL have created it Some philosophers have answered this question by saying that THE ALL created the Universe from ITSELF—that is, from the being and substance of THE ALL. But this will not do, for THE ALL cannot be subtracted from, nor divided, as we have seen, and then again if this be so, would not each particle in the Universe be aware of its being THE ALL—THE ALL could not lose its knowledge of itself, nor actually BECOME an atom, or blind force, or lowly living thing. Some men, indeed, realizing that THE ALL is indeed ALL, and also recognizing that they, the men, existed, have jumped to the conclusion that they and THE ALL were identical, and they have filled the air with shouts of "I AM GOD," to the amusement of the multitude and the sorrow of sages. The claim of the corpuscle that: "I am Man!" would be

modest in comparison. But, what indeed is the Universe, if it be not THE ALL, not yet created by THE ALL having separated itself into fragments? What else can it be of what else can it be made? This is the great question. Let us examine it carefully. We find here that the "Principle of Correspondence" (see Lesson I.) comes to our aid here. The old Hermetic axiom, "As above so below," may be pressed into service at this point. Let us endeavor to get a glimpse of the workings on higher planes by examining those on our own. The Principle of Correspondence must apply to this as well as to other problems.

Let us see! On his own plane of being, how does Man create? Well, first, he may create by making something out of outside materials. But this will not do, for there are no materials outside of THE ALL with which it may create. Well, then, secondly, Man pro-creates or reproduces his kind by the process of begetting, which is self-multiplication accomplished by transferring a portion of his substance to his offspring. But this will not do, because THE ALL cannot transfer or subtract a portion of itself, nor can it reproduce or multiply itself—in the first place there would be a taking away, and in the second case a multiplication or addition to THE ALL, both thoughts being an absurdity. Is there no third way in which MAN creates? Yes, there is—he CREATES MENTALLY! And in so doing he uses no outside materials, nor does he reproduce himself, and yet his Spirit pervades the Mental Creation. Following the Principle of Correspondence, we are justified in considering that THE ALL creates the Universe MENTALLY, in a manner akin to the process whereby Man creates Mental Images. And, here is where the report of Reason tallies precisely with the report of the Illumined, as shown by their teachings and writings. Such are the teachings of the Wise Men. Such was the Teaching of Hermes. THE ALL can create in no other way except mentally, without either using material (and there is none to use), or else reproducing itself (which is also impossible). There is no escape from this conclusion of the Reason, which, as we have said, agrees with the highest teachings of the Illumined. Just as you, student, may create a Universe of your own in your mentality, so does THE ALL create Universes in its own Mentality. But your Universe is the mental creation of a Finite Mind, whereas that of THE ALL is the creation of an Infinite. The two are similar in kind, but infinitely different in degree. We shall examine more closely into the process of creation and manifestation as we proceed. But this is the point to fix in your minds at this stage: THE UNIVERSE, AND ALL IT CONTAINS, IS A MENTAL CREATION OF THE ALL. Verily indeed, ALL IS MIND!

"THE ALL creates in its Infinite Mind countless Universes, which exist for aeons of Time—and yet, to THE ALL, the creation, development, decline and death of a million Universes is as the time of the twinkling of an eye."—*The Kybalion.*
"The Infinite Mind of THE ALL is the womb of Universes."—*The Kybalion.*

The Principle of Gender (see Lesson I. and other lessons to follow) is manifested on all planes of life, material mental and spiritual. But, as we have said before, "Gender" does not mean "Sex" sex is merely a material manifestation of gender. "Gender" means "relating to generation or creation." And whenever anything is generated or created, on any plane, the Principle of Gender must be manifested. And this is true even in the creation of Universes.

Now do not jump to the conclusion that we are teaching that there is a male and female God, or Creator. That idea is merely a distortion of the ancient teachings on the subject. The true teaching is that THE ALL, in itself, is above Gender, as it is above every other Law, including those of Time and Space. It is the Law, from which the Laws proceed, and it is not subject to them. But when THE ALL manifests on the plane of generation or creation, then it acts according to Law and Principle, for it is moving on a lower plane of Being. And consequently it manifests the Principle of Gender, in its Masculine and Feminine aspects, on the Mental Plane, of course.

This idea may seem startling to some of you who hear it for the first time, but you have all really passively accepted it in your everyday conceptions. You speak of the Fatherhood of God, and the Motherhood of Nature—of God, the Divine Father, and Nature the Universal Mother—and have thus instinctively acknowledged the Principle of Gender in the Universe. Is this not so?

But, the Hermetic teaching does not imply a real duality—THE ALL is ONE the Two Aspects are merely aspects of manifestation. The teaching is that The Masculine Principle manifested by THE ALL stands, in a way, apart from the actual mental creation of the Universe. It projects its Will toward the Feminine Principle (which may be called "Nature") whereupon the latter begins the actual work of the evolution of the Universe, from simple "centers of activity" on to man, and then on and on still higher, all according to well-established and firmly enforced Laws of Nature. If you prefer the old figures of thought, you may think of the Masculine Principle as GOD, the Father, and of the Feminine Principle as NATURE, the Universal Mother, from whose womb all things have been born. This is more than a mere poetic figure of speech—it is an idea of the actual process of the creation of the Universe. But always remember, that THE ALL is but One, and that in

its Infinite Mind the Universe is generated, created and exists.

It may help you to get the proper idea, if you will apply the Law of Correspondence to yourself, and your own mind. You know that the part of You which you call "I," in a sense, stands apart and witnesses the creation of mental Images in your own mind. The part of your mind in which the mental generation is accomplished may be called the "Me" in distinction from the "I" which stands apart and witnesses and examines the thoughts, ideas and images of the "Me."

"As above, so below," remember, and the phenomena of one plane may be employed to solve the riddles of higher or lower planes.

Is it any wonder that You, the child, feel that instinctive reverence for THE ALL, which feeling we call "religion"—that respect, and reverence for THE FATHER MIND? Is it any wonder that, when you consider the works and wonders of Nature, you are overcome with a mighty feeling which has its roots away down in your inmost being? It is the MOTHER MIND that you are pressing close up to, like a babe to the breast.

Do not make the mistake of supposing that the little world you see around you—the Earth, which is a mere grain of dust in the Universe—is the Universe itself. There are millions upon millions of such worlds, and greater. And there are millions of millions of such Universes in existence within the Infinite Mind of THE ALL. And even in our own little solar system there are regions and planes of life far higher than ours, and beings compared to which we earth-bound mortals are as the slimy life-forms that dwell on the ocean's bed when compared to Man. There are beings with powers and attributes higher than Man has ever dreamed of the gods' possessing. And yet these beings were once as you, and still lower—and you will be even as they, and still higher, in time, for such is the Destiny of Man as reported by the Illumined.

And Death is not real, even in the Relative sense—it is but Birth to a new life—and You shall go on, and on, and on, to higher and still higher planes of life, for aeons upon aeons of time. The Universe is your home, and you shall explore its farthest recesses before the end of Time. You are dwelling in the Infinite Mind of THE ALL, and your possibilities and opportunities are infinite, both in time and space. And at the end of the Grand Cycle of Aeons, when THE ALL shall draw back into itself all of its creations—you will go gladly for you will then be able to know the Whole Truth of being At One with THE ALL. Such is the report of the Illumined—those who have advanced well along The Path.

And, in the meantime, rest calm and serene—you are safe and protected by the Infinite Power of the FATHER-MOTHER MIND.

"Within the Father-Mother Mind, mortal children are at home."—*The Kybalion*

"There is not one who is Fatherless, nor Motherless in the Universe."—*The Kybalion*

Chapter VI. *The Divine Paradox*

"The half-wise, recognizing the comparative unreality of the Universe, imagine that they may defy its Laws—such are vain and presumptuous fools, and they are broken against the rocks and torn asunder by the elements by reason of their folly. The truly wise, knowing the nature of the Universe, use Law against laws; the higher against the lower; and by the Art of Alchemy transmute that which is undesirable into that which is worthy, and thus triumph. Mastery consists not in abnormal dreams, visions and fantastic imaginings or living, but in using the higher forces against the lower—escaping the pains of the lower planes by vibrating on the higher. Transmutation, not presumptuous denial, is the weapon of the Master."—*The Kybalion.*

This is the Paradox of the Universe, resulting from the Principle of Polarity which manifests when THE ALL begins to Create—hearken to it for it points the difference between half-wisdom and wisdom. While to THE INFINITE ALL, the Universe, its Laws, its Powers, its life, its Phenomena, are as things witnessed in the state of Meditation or Dream; yet to all that is Finite, the Universe must be treated as Real, and life, and action, and thought, must be based thereupon, accordingly, although with an ever understanding of the Higher Truth. Each according to its own Plane and Laws. Were THE ALL to imagine that the Universe were indeed Reality, then woe to the Universe, for there would be then no escape from lower to higher, divineward—then would the Universe become a fixity and progress would become impossible. And if Man, owing to half-wisdom, acts and lives and thinks of the Universe as merely a dream (akin to his own finite dreams) then indeed does it so become for him, and like a sleep-walker he stumbles ever around and around in a circle, making no progress, and being forced into an awakening at last by his falling bruised and bleeding over the Natural Laws which he ignored. Keep your mind ever on the Star, but let your eyes watch over your footsteps, lest you fall into the mire by reason of your upward gaze. Remember the Divine Paradox, that while the Universe IS NOT, still IT IS. Remember ever the Two Poles of Truth the Absolute and the Relative. Beware of Half-Truths.

What Hermetists know as "the Law of Paradox" is an aspect of the Principle of Polarity. The Hermetic writings are filled with references to the appearance of the Paradox in the consideration of the problems of Life and Being. The Teachers are constantly warning their students against the error of omitting the "other side" of any question. And their warnings are particularly directed to the problems of the Absolute and the Relative, which perplex all students of philosophy, and which cause

so many to think and act contrary to what is generally known as "common sense." And we caution all students to be sure to grasp the Divine Paradox of the Absolute and Relative, lest they become entangled in the mire of the Half-Truth. With this in view this particular lesson has been written. Read it carefully!

The first thought that comes to the thinking man after he realizes the truth that the Universe is a Mental Creation of THE ALL, is that the Universe and all that it contains is a mere illusion; an unreality; against which idea his instincts revolt. But this, like all other great truths, must be considered both from the Absolute and the Relative points of view. From the Absolute viewpoint, of course, the Universe is in the nature of an illusion, a dream, a phantasmagoria, as compared to THE ALL in itself. We recognize this even in our ordinary view, for we speak of the world as "a fleeting show" that comes and goes, is born and dies—for the element of impermanence and change, finiteness and unsubstantiality, must ever be connected with the idea of a created Universe when it is contrasted with the idea of THE ALL, no matter what may be our beliefs concerning the nature of both. Philosopher, metaphysician, scientist and theologian all agree upon this idea, and the thought is found in all forms of philosophical thought and religious conceptions, as well as in the theories of the respective schools of metaphysics and theology. So, the Hermetic Teachings do not preach the unsubstantiality of the Universe in any stronger terms than those more familiar to you, although their presentation of the subject may seem somewhat more startling. Anything that has a beginning and an ending must be, in a sense, unreal and untrue, and the Universe comes under the rule, in all schools of thought. From the Absolute point of view, there is nothing Real except THE ALL, no matter what terms we may use in thinking of, or discussing the subject. Whether the Universe be created of Matter, or whether it be a Mental Creation in the Mind of THE ALL—it is unsubstantial, non-enduring, a thing of time, space and change. We want you to realize this fact thoroughly, before you pass judgment on the Hermetic conception of the Mental nature of the Universe. Think over any and all of the other conceptions, and see whether this be not true of them.

But the Absolute point of view shows merely one side of the picture—the other side is the Relative one. Absolute Truth has been defined as "Things as the mind of God knows them," while Relative Truth is "Things as the highest reason of Man understands them." And so while to THE ALL the Universe must be unreal and illusionary, a mere dream or result of meditation,—nevertheless, to the finite minds forming a part of that Universe, and viewing it through mortal faculties, the Universe is very real indeed, and must be so considered. In recognizing the Absolute view, we must not make the mistake of ignoring or denying the facts and phenomena of the Universe as they

present themselves to our mortal faculties—we are not THE ALL, remember.

To take familiar illustrations, we all recognize the fact that matter "exists" to our senses—we will fare badly if we do not. And yet, even our finite minds understand the scientific dictum that there is no such thing as Matter from a scientific point of view—that which we call Matter is held to be merely an aggregation of atoms, which atoms themselves are merely a grouping of units of force, called electrons or "ions," vibrating and in constant circular motion. We kick a stone and we feel the impact—it seems to be real, notwithstanding that we know it to be merely what we have stated above. But remember that our foot, which feels the impact by means of our brains, is likewise Matter, so constituted of electrons, and for that matter so are our brains. And, at the best, if it were not by reason of our Mind, we would not know the foot or stone at all.

Then again, the ideal of the artist or sculptor, which he is endeavoring to reproduce in stone or on canvas, seems very real to him. So do the characters in the mind of the author; or dramatist, which he seeks to express so that others may recognize them. And if this be true in the case of our finite minds, what must be the degree of Reality in the Mental Images created in the Mind of the Infinite? Oh, friends, to mortals this Universe of Mentality is very real indeed—it is the only one we can ever know, though we rise from plane to plane, higher and higher in it. To know it otherwise, but actual experience, we must be THE ALL itself. It is true that the higher we rise in the nearer to "the mind of the Father" we reach—the more apparent becomes the illusory nature of finite things, but not until THE ALL finally withdraws us into itself does the vision actually vanish.

So, we need not dwell upon the feature of illusion. Rather let us, recognizing the real nature of the Universe, seek to understand its mental laws, and endeavor to use them to the best effect in our upward progress through life, as we travel from plane to plane of being. The Laws of the Universe are none the less "Iron Laws" because of the mental nature. All, except THE ALL, are bound by them. What is IN THE INFINITE MIND OF THE all; is REAL in a degree second only to that Reality itself which is vested in the nature of THE ALL.

So, do not feel insecure or afraid—we are all HELD FIRMLY IN THE INFINITE MIND OF THE ALL, and there is naught to hurt us or for us to fear. There is no Power outside of THE ALL to affect us. So we may rest calm and secure. There is a world of comfort and security in this realization when once attained. Then "calm and peaceful do we sleep, rocked in the Cradle of the Deep"—resting safely on the bosom of the Ocean of Infinite Mind, which is THE ALL. In THE ALL, indeed, do "we live and move and have our being."

Matter is none the less Matter to us, while we dwell on the plane of

Matter, although we know it to be merely an aggregation of "electrons," or particles of Force, vibrating rapidly and gyrating around each other in the formations of atoms; the atoms in turn vibrating and gyrating, forming molecules, which latter in turn form larger masses of Matter. Nor does Matter become less Matter, when we follow the inquiry still further, and learn from the Hermetic Teachings, that the "Force" of which the electrons are but units is merely a manifestation of the Mind of THE ALL, and like all else in the Universe is purely Mental in its nature. While on the Plane of matter, we must recognize its phenomena—we may control Matter (as all Masters of higher or lesser degree do), but we do so by applying the higher forces. We commit a folly when we attempt to deny the existence of Matter in the relative aspect. We may deny its mastery over us—and rightly so—but we should not attempt to ignore it in its relative aspect, at least so long as we dwell upon its plane.

Nor do the Laws of Nature become less constant or effective, when we know them, likewise, to be merely mental creations. They are in full effect on the various planes. We overcome the lower laws, by applying still higher ones—and in this way only. But we cannot escape Law or rise above it entirely. Nothing but THE ALL can escape Law—and that because THE ALL is LAW itself, from which all Laws emerge. The most advanced Masters may acquire the powers usually attributed to the gods of men; and there are countless ranks of being, in the great hierarchy of life, whose being and power transcends even that of the highest Masters among men to a degree unthinkable by mortals, but even the highest Master, and the highest Being, must bow to the Law, and be as Nothing in the eye of THE ALL. So that if even these highest Beings, whose powers exceed even those attributed by men to their gods—if even these are bound by and are subservient to Law, then imagine the presumption of mortal man, of our race and grade, when he dares to consider the Laws of Nature as "unreal!" visionary and illusory, because he happens to be able to grasp the truth that the Laws are Mental in nature, and simply Mental Creations of THE ALL. Those Laws which THE ALL intends to be governing Laws are not to be defied or argued away. So long as the Universe endures, will they endure—for the Universe exists by virtue of these Laws which form its framework and which hold it together.

The Hermetic Principle of Mentalism, while explaining the true nature of the Universe upon the principle that all is Mental, does not change the scientific conceptions of the Universe, Life, or Evolution. In fact, science merely corroborates the Hermetic Teachings. The latter merely teaches that the nature of the Universe is "Mental," while modern science has taught that it is "Material"; or (of late) that it is "Energy" at the last analysis. The Hermetic Teachings have no fault to find with Herbert Spencer's basic principle which postulates the

existence of an "<u>Infinite and Eternal Energy, from which all things proceed</u>." In fact, the Hermetics recognize in Spencer's philosophy the highest outside statement of the workings of the Natural Laws that have ever been promulgated, and they believe Spencer to have been a reincarnation of an ancient philosopher who dwelt in ancient Egypt thousands of years ago, and who later incarnated as Heraclitus, the Grecian philosopher who lived B. C. 500. And they regard his statement of the "Infinite and Eternal Energy" as directly in the line of the Hermetic Teachings, always with the addition of their own doctrine that his "Energy" is the Energy of the Mind of THE ALL. With the Master-Key of the Hermetic Philosophy, the student of Spencer will be able to unlock many doors of the inner philosophical conceptions of the great English philosopher, whose work shows the results of the preparation of his previous incarnations. His teachings regarding Evolution and Rhythm are in almost perfect agreement with the Hermetic Teachings regarding the Principle of Rhythm.

So, the student of Hermetics need not lay aside any of his cherished scientific views regarding the Universe. All he is asked to do is to grasp the underlying principle of "<u>THE ALL is Mind; the Universe is Mental—held in the mind of THE ALL</u>." He will find that the other six of the Seven Principles will "fit into" his scientific knowledge, and will serve to bring out obscure points and to throw light in dark corners. This is not to be wondered at, when we realize the influence of the Hermetic thought of the early philosophers of Greece, upon whose foundations of thought the theories of modern science largely rest. The acceptance of the First Hermetic Principle (Mentalism is the only great point of difference between Modern Science and Hermetic students, and Science is gradually moving toward the Hermetic position in its groping in the dark for a way out of the Labyrinth into which it has wandered in its search for Reality.

The purpose of this lesson is to impress upon the minds of our students the fact that, to all intents and purposes, the Universe and its laws, and its phenomena, are just as REAL, so far as Man is concerned as they would be under the hypotheses of Materialism or Energism. Under any hypothesis the Universe in its outer aspect is changing, ever-flowing, and transitory—and therefore devoid of substantiality and reality. But (note the other pole of the truth) under the same hypotheses, <u>we are compelled to ACT AND LIVE as if the fleeting things were real and substantial</u>. With this difference, always, between the various hypotheses—that under the old views Mental Power was ignored as a Natural Force, while under Mentalism it becomes the Greatest Natural Force. and this one difference revolutionizes Life, to those who understand the Principle and its resulting laws and practice.

So, finally, students all, grasp the advantage of Mentalism, and learn to know, use and apply the laws resulting therefrom. But do not

yield to the temptation which, as The Kybalion states, overcomes the half-wise and which causes them to be hypnotized by the apparent unreality of things, the consequence being that they wander about like dream-people dwelling in a world of dreams, ignoring the practical work and life of man, the end being that "they are broken against the rocks and torn asunder by the elements, by reason of their folly." Rather follow the example of the wise, which the same authority states, "use Law against Laws; the higher against the lower; and by the Art of Alchemy transmute that which is undesirable into that which is worthy, and thus triumph." Following the authority, let us avoid the half-wisdom (which is folly) which ignores the truth that: "Mastery consists not in abnormal dreams, visions, and fantastic imaginings or living, but in using the higher forces against the lower-escaping the pains of the lower planes by vibrating on the higher." Remember always, student, that "Transmutation, not presumptuous denial, is the weapon of the Master." The above quotations are from The Kybalion, and are worthy of being committed to memory by the student.

We do not live in a world of dreams, but in an Universe which while relative, is real so far as our lives and actions are concerned. Our business in the Universe is not to deny its existence, but to LIVE, using the Laws to rise from lower to higher-living on, doing the best that we can under the circumstances arising each day, and living, so far as is possible, to our biggest ideas and ideals. The true Meaning of Life is not known to men on this plane .if, indeed, to any—but the highest authorities, and our own intuitions, teach us that we will make no mistake in living up to the best that is in us, so far as is possible, and realising the Universal tendency in the same direction in spite of apparent evidence to the contrary. We are all on The Path—and the road leads upward ever, with frequent resting places.

Read the message of The Kybalion—and follow the example of "the wise"—avoiding the mistake of "the half-wise" who perish by reason of their folly.

Chapter VII. "The All" in All

"While All is in THE ALL, it is equally true that THE ALL is in ALL. To him who truly understands this truth hath come great knowledge."—*The Kybalion*

How often have the majority of people heard repeated the statement that their Deity (called by many names) was "All in All" and how little have they suspected the inner occult truth concealed by these carelessly uttered words? The commonly used expression is a survival of the ancient. Hermetic Maxim quoted above. as the Kybalion says: "To him who truly understands this truth, hath come great knowledge." And, this being so, let us seek this truth, the understanding of which means so much. In this statement of truth—this Hermetic Maxim—is concealed one of the greatest philosophical, scientific and religious truths.

We have given you the Hermetic Teaching regarding the Mental Nature of the Universe—the truth that "the Universe is Mental—held in the Mind of THE ALL" As the Kybalion says, in the passage quoted above: "All is in THE ALL." But note also the co-related statement, that: "It is equally true that THE ALL is in ALL." This apparently contradictory statement is reconcilable under the Law of Paradox. It is, moreover, an exact Hermetic statement of the relations existing between THE ALL and its mental Universe. We have seen how "All is in THE ALL"—now let us examine the other aspect of the subject.

The Hermetic Teachings are to the effect that THE ALL is Imminent in ("remaining within; inherent; abiding within") its Universe, and in every part, particle, unit, or combination, within the Universe. This statement is usually illustrated by the Teachers by a reference to the Principle of Correspondence. The Teacher instructs the student to form a Mental Image of something, a person, an idea, something having a mental form, the favorite example being that of the author or dramatist forming an idea of his characters; or a painter or sculptor forming an image of an ideal that he wishes to express by his art. In each case, the student will find that while the image has its existence, and being, solely within his own mind, yet he, the student, author, dramatist, painter, or sculptor, is, in a sense, immanent in; remaining within; or abiding within, the mental image also. In other words, the entire virtue, life, spirit, of reality in the mental image is derived from the "immanent mind" of the thinker. Consider this for a moment, until the idea is grasped.

To take a modern example, let us say that Othello, Iago, Hamlet, Lear, Richard III, existed merely in the mind of Shakespeare, at the time of their conception or creation. And yet, Shakespeare also existed

within each of these characters, giving them their vitality, spirit, and action. Whose is the "spirit" of the characters that we know as Micawber, Oliver Twist, Uriah Heep—is it Dickens, or have each of these characters a personal spirit, independent of their creator? Have the Venus of Medici, the Sistine Madonna, the Appollo Belvidere, spirits and reality of their own, or do they represent the spiritual and mental power of their creators? The Law of Paradox explains that both propositions are true, viewed from the proper viewpoints. Micawber is both Micawber, and yet Dickens. And, again, while Micawber may be said to be Dickens, yet Dickens is not identical with Micawber. Man, like Micawber, may exclaim: "The Spirit of my Creator is inherent within me—and yet I: am not HE!" How different this from the shocking half-truth so vociferously announced by certain of the half wise, who fill the air with their raucous cries of: "I am God!" Imagine poor Micawber, or the sneaky Uriah Heep, crying: "I Am Dickens"; or some of the lowly clods in one of Shakespeare's plays, eloquently announcing that: I Am Shakespeare!" THE ALL is in the earthworm, and yet the earthworm is far from being THE ALL. And still the wonder remains, that though the earthworm exists merely as a lowly thing, created and having its being solely within the Mind of THE ALL—yet THE ALL is immanent in the earthworm, and in the particles that go to make up the earthworm. Can there be any greater mystery than this of "All in THE ALL; and THE ALL in All?"

The student will, of course, realize that the illustrations given above are necessarily imperfect and inadequate, for they represent the creation of mental images in finite minds, while the Universe is a creation of Infinite Mind—and the difference between the two poles separates them. And yet it is merely a matter of degree—the same Principle is in operation—the Principle of Correspondence manifests in each—"As above, so Below; as Below, so above."

And, in the degree that Man realizes the existence of the Indwelling Spirit immanent within his being, so will he rise in the spiritual scale of life. This is what spiritual development means—the recognition, realization, and manifestation of the Spirit within us. Try to remember this last definition—that of spiritual development. It contains the Truth of True Religion.

There are many planes of Being—many sub-planes of Life—many degrees of existence in the Universe. And all depend upon the advancement of beings in the scale, of which scale the lowest point is the grossest matter, the highest being separated only by the thinnest division from the SPIRIT of THE ALL. And, upward and onward along this Scale of Life, everything is moving. All are on the Path, whose end is THE ALL. All progress is a Returning Home. All is Upward and Onward, in spite of all seemingly contradictory appearances. Such is the message of the illumined.

The Hermetic Teachings concerning the process of the Mental Creation of the Universe, are that at the beginning of the Creative Cycle, THE ALL, in its aspect of Being, projects its Will toward its aspect of "Becoming" and the process of creation begins. It is taught that the process consists of the lowering of Vibration until a very low degree of vibratory energy is reached, at which point the grossest possible form of Matter is manifested. This process is called the stage of Involution, in which THE ALL becomes "involved," or "wrapped up," in its creation. This process is believed by the Hermetists to have a Correspondence to the mental process of an artist, writer, or inventor, who becomes so wrapped up in his mental creation as to almost forget his own existence and who, for the time being, almost "lives in his creation," If instead of "wrapped" we use the word "rapt," perhaps we will give a better idea of what is meant.

This Involuntary stage of Creation is sometimes called the "Outpouring" of the Divine Energy, just as the Evolutionary state is called the "Indrawing." The extreme pole of the Creative process is considered to be the furthest removed from THE ALL, while the beginning of the Evolutionary stage is regarded as the beginning of the return swing of the pendulum of Rhythm—a "coming home" idea being held in all of the Hermetic Teachings.

The Teachings are that during the "Outpouring," the vibrations become lower and lower until finally the urge ceases, and the return swing begins. But there is this difference, that while in the "Outpouring" the creative forces manifest compactly and as a whole, yet from the beginning of the Evolutionary or "Indrawing" stage, there is manifested the Law of Individualization—that is, the tendency to separate into Units of Force, so that finally that which left THE ALL as unindividualized energy returns to its source as countless highly developed Units of Life, having risen higher and higher in the scale by means of Physical, Mental and Spiritual Evolution.

The ancient Hermetists use the word "Meditation" in describing the process of the mental creation of the Universe in the Mind of THE ALL, the word "Contemplation" also being frequently employed. But the idea intended seems to be that of the employment of the Divine Attention. "Attention" is a word derived from the Latin root, meaning "to reach out; to stretch out," and so the act of Attention is really a mental "reaching out; extension" of mental energy, so that the underlying idea is readily understood when we examine into the real meaning of "Attention."

The Hermetic Teachings regarding the process of Evolution are that, THE ALL, having meditated upon the beginning of the Creation—having thus established the material foundations of the Universe having thought it into existence—then gradually awakens or rouses from its Meditation and in so doing starts into manifestation the process of

Evolution, on the material mental and spiritual planes, successively and in order. Thus the upward movement begins—and all begins to move Spiritward. Matter becomes less gross; the Units spring into being; the combinations begin to form; Life appears and manifests in higher and higher forms. and Mind becomes more and more in evidence—the vibrations constantly becoming higher. In short, the entire process of Evolution, in all of its phases, begins, and proceeds according to the established Laws of the Indrawing" process. All of this occupies aeons upon aeons of Man's time, each aeon containing countless millions of years, but yet the Illumined inform us that the entire creation, including Involution and Evolution, of an Universe, is but "as the twinkle of the eye" to THE ALL At the end of countless cycles of aeons of time, THE ALL withdraws its Attention—its Contemplation and Meditation—of the Universe, for the Great Work is finished—and All is withdrawn into THE ALL from which it emerged. But Mystery of Mysteries—the Spirit of each soul is not annihilated, but is infinitely expanded—the Created and the Creator are merged. Such is the report of the Illumined.

The above illustration of the "meditation," and subsequent "awakening from meditation," of THE ALL, is of course but an attempt of the teachers to describe the Infinite process by a finite example. And, yet: "As Below, so Above." The difference is merely in degree. And just. as THE ALL arouses itself from the meditation upon the Universe, so does Man (in time) cease from manifesting upon the Material Plane, and withdraws himself more and more into the Indwelling Spirit, which is indeed "The Divine Ego."

There is one more matter of which we desire to speak in this lesson, and that comes very near to an invasion of the Metaphysical field of speculation, although our purpose is merely to show the futility of such speculation. We allude to the question which inevitably comes to the mind of all thinkers who have ventured to seek the Truth. The question is: "WHY does THE ALL create Universes" The question may be asked in different forms, but the above is the gist of the inquiry.

Men have striven hard to answer this question, but still there is no answer worthy of the name. Some have imagined that THE ALL had something to gain by it, but this is absurd, for what could THE ALL gain that it did not already possess? Others have sought the answer in the idea that THE ALL "wished something to love" and others that it created for pleasure, or amusement; or because it "was lonely" or to manifest its power;—all puerile explanations and ideas, belonging to the childish period of thought.

Others have sought to explain the mystery by assuming that THE ALL found itself "compelled" to create, by reason of its own "internal nature" its "creative instinct." This idea is in advance of the others, but its weak point lies in the idea of THE ALL being "compelled" by anything, internal or external. If its "internal nature," or "creative

instinct," compelled it to do anything, then the "internal nature" or "creative instinct" would be the Absolute, instead of THE ALL, and so accordingly that part of the proposition falls. And, yet, THE ALL does create and manifest, and seems to find some kind of satisfaction in so doing. And it is difficult to escape the conclusion that in some infinite degree it must have what would correspond to an "inner nature," or "creative instinct," in man, with correspondingly infinite Desire and Will. It could not act unless it Willed to Act; and it would not Will to Act, unless it Desired to Act and it would not Desire to Act unless it obtained some Satisfaction thereby. And all of these things would belong to an "Inner Nature," and might be postulated as existing according to the Law of Correspondence. But, still, we prefer to think of THE ALL as acting entirely FREE from any influence, internal as well as external. That is the problem which lies at the root of difficulty—and the difficulty that lies at the root of the problem.

Strictly speaking, there cannot be said to be any "Reason" whatsoever for THE ALL to act, for a "reason" implies a "cause," and THE ALL is above Cause and Effect, except when it Wills to become a Cause, at which time the Principle is set into motion. So, you see, the matter is Unthinkable, just as THE ALL is Unknowable. Just as we say THE ALL merely "IS"—so we are compelled to say that "THE ALL ACTS BECAUSE IT ACTS." At the last, THE ALL is All Reason in Itself; All Law in Itself; All Action in Itself—and it may be said, truthfully, that THE ALL is Its Own Reason; its own Law; its own Act—or still further, that THE ALL; Its Reason; Its Act; is Law; are ONE, all being names for the same thing. In the opinion of those who are giving you these present lessons, the answer is locked up in the INNER SELF of THE ALL, along with its Secret of Being. The Law of Correspondence, in our opinion, reaches only to that aspect of THE ALL, which may be spoken of as "The Aspect of BECOMING." Back of that Aspect is "The Aspect of BEING " in which all Laws are lost in LAW; all Principles merge into PRINCIPLE—and THE ALL ; PRINCIPLE ; and BEING ; are IDENTICAL, ONE AND THE SAME. Therefore, Metaphysical speculation on this point is futile. We go into the matter here, merely to show that we recognize the question, and also the absurdity of the ordinary answers of metaphysics and theology.

In conclusion, it may be of interest to our students to learn that while some of the ancient, and modern, Hermetic Teachers have rather inclined in the direction of applying the Principle of Correspondence to the question, with the result of the "Inner Nature" conclusion,—still the legends have it that HERMES, the Great, when asked this question by his advanced students, answered them by PRESSING HIS LIPS TIGHTLY TOGETHER and saying not a word, indicating that there WAS NO ANSWER. But, then, he may have intended to apply the axiom of his philosophy, that: "The lips of Wisdom are closed, except

to the ears of Understanding," believing that even his advanced students did not possess the Understanding which entitled them to the Teaching. At any rate, if Hermes possessed the Secret, he failed to impart it, and so far as the world is concerned THE LIPS OF HERMES ARE CLOSED regarding it. And where the Great Hermes hesitated to speak, what mortal may dare to teach?

But, remember, that whatever be the answer to this problem, if indeed there be an answer the truth remains that "While All is in THE ALL, it is equally true that THE ALL is in All." The Teaching on this point is emphatic. And, we may add the concluding words of the quotation: "To him who truly understands this truth, hath come great knowledge."

Chapter VIII. The Planes of Correspondence

"As above, so below; as below, so above."—*The Kybalion.*

The great Second Hermetic Principle embodies the truth that there is a harmony, agreement, and correspondence between the several planes of Manifestation, Life and Being. This truth is a truth because all that is included in the Universe emanates from the same source, and the same laws, principles, and characteristics apply to each unit, or combination of unit, of activity, as each manifests its own phenomena upon its own plane.

For the purpose of convenience of thought and study, the Hermetic Philosophy considers that the Universe may be divided into three great classes of phenomena, known as the Three Great Planes, namely:

I. The Great Physical Plane.
II. The Great Mental Plane.
III. The Great Spiritual Plane.

These divisions are more or less artificial and arbitrary, for the truth is that all of the three divisions are but ascending degrees of the great scale of Life, the lowest point of which is undifferentiated Matter, and the highest point that of Spirit. And, moreover, the different Planes shade into each other, so that no hard and fast division may be made between the higher phenomena of the Physical and the lower of the Mental; or between the higher of the Mental and the lower of the Physical.

In short, the Three Great Planes may be regarded as three great groups of degrees of Life Manifestation. While the purposes of this little book do not allow us to enter into an extended discussion of, or explanation of, the subject of these different planes, still we think it well to give a general description of the same at this point.

At the beginning we may as well consider the question so often asked by the neophyte, who desires to be informed regarding the meaning of the word Plane, which term has been very freely used, and very poorly explained, in many recent works upon the subject of occultism. The question is generally about as follows: Is a Plane a place having dimensions, or is it merely a condition or state?" We answer: "No, not a place, nor ordinary dimension of space; and yet more than a state or condition. It may be considered as a state or condition, and yet the state or condition is a degree of dimension, in a scale subject to measurement. "Somewhat paradoxical, is it not? But let us examine the matter. A "dimension," you know, is "a measure in a straight line, relating to measure," etc. The ordinary dimensions of space are length,

breadth, and height, or perhaps length, breadth, height, thickness or circumference. But there is another dimension of "created things" or "measure," known to occultists, and to scientists as well, although the latter have not as yet applied the term "dimension" to it and this new dimension, which, by the way, is the much speculated-about "Fourth Dimension," is the standard used in determining the degrees or "planes."

This Fourth Dimension may be called "The Dimension of Vibration" It is a fact well known to modern science, as well as to the Hermetists who have embodied the truth in their "Third Hermetic Principle," that everything is in motion; everything vibrates; nothing is at rest. From the highest manifestation, to the lowest, everything and all things Vibrate. Not only do they vibrate at different rates of motion, but as in different directions and in a different manner. The degrees of the rate of vibrations constitute the degrees of measurement on the Scale of Vibrations—in other words the degrees of the Fourth Dimension. And these degrees form what occultists call "Planes" The higher the degree of rate of vibration, the higher the plane, and the higher the manifestation of Life occupying that plane. So that while a plane is not "a place," nor yet "a state or condition," yet it possesses qualities common to both. We shall have more to say regarding the subject of the scale of Vibrations in our next lessons, in which we shall consider the Hermetic Principle of Vibration.

You will kindly remember, however, that the Three Great Planes are not actual divisions of the phenomena of the Universe, but merely arbitrary terms used by the Hermetists in order to aid in the thought and study of the various degrees and Forms of universal activity and life. The atom of matter, the unit of force, the mind of man, and the being of the arch-angel are all but degrees in one scale, and all fundamentally the same, the difference between solely a matter of degree, and rate of vibration—all are creations of THE ALL, and have their existence solely within the Infinite Mind of THE ALL.

The Hermetists sub-divide each of the Three Great Planes into Seven Minor Planes, and each of these latter are also sub-divided into seven sub-planes, all divisions being more or less arbitrary, shading into each other, and adopted merely for convenience of scientific study and thought. The Great Physical Plane, and its Seven Minor Planes, is that division of the phenomena of the Universe which includes all that relates to physics, or material things, forces, and manifestations. It includes all forms of that which we call Matter, and all forms of that which we call Energy or Force. But you must remember that the Hermetic Philosophy does not recognize Matter as a thing in itself, or as having a separate existence even in the Mind of THE ALL. The Teachings are that Matter is but a form of Energy—.that is, Energy at a low rate of vibrations of a certain kind. And accordingly the Hermetists

classify Matter under the head of Energy, and give to it three of the Seven Minor Planes of the Great Physical Plane.

These Seven Minor Physical Planes are as follows:

> I. The Plane of Matter (A)
> II. The Plane of Matter (B)
> III. The Plane of Matter (C)
> IV. The Plane of Ethereal Substance.
> V. The Plane of Energy (A)
> VI. The Plane of Energy (B)
> VII. The Plane of Energy (C)

The Plane of Matter (A) comprises forms of Matter in its form of solids, liquids, and gases, as generally recognized by the text-books on physics. The Plane of Matter (B) comprises certain higher and more subtle forms of Matter of the existence of which modern science is but now recognizing, the phenomena of Radiant Matter, in its phases of radium, etc., belonging to the lower sub-division of this Minor Plane. The Plane of Matter (C) comprises forms of the most subtle and tenuous Matter, the existence of which is not suspected by ordinary scientists. The Plane of Ethereal Substance comprises that which science speaks of as The Ether, a substance of extreme tenuity and elasticity, pervading all Universal Space, and acting as a medium for the transmission of waves of energy, such as light, heat, electricity, etc. This Ethereal Substance forms a connecting link between Matter (so-called) and Energy, and partakes of the nature of each. The Hermetic Teachings, however, instruct that this plane has seven sub-divisions (as have all of the Minor Planes), and that in fact there are seven ethers, instead of but one.

Next above the Plane of Ethereal Substance comes the Plane of Energy (A), which comprises the ordinary forms of Energy known to science, its seven sub planes being, respectively, Heat; Light; Magnetism; Electricity, and Attraction (including Gravitation, Cohesion, Chemical Affinity, etc.) and several other forms of energy indicated by scientific experiments but not as yet named or classified. The Plane of Energy (B) comprises seven sub-planes of higher forms of energy not as yet discovered by science, but which have been called "Nature's Finer Forces" and which are called into operation in manifestations of certain forms of mental phenomena, and by which such phenomena becomes possible. The Plane of Energy (C) comprises seven sub-planes of energy so highly organized that it bears many of the characteristics of "life," but which is not recognized by the minds of men on the ordinary plane of development, being available for the use on beings of the Spiritual Plane alone—such energy is unthinkable to

ordinary man, and may be considered almost as "the divine power." The beings employing the same are as "gods" compared even to the highest human types known to us.

The Great Mental Plane comprises those forms of "living things" known to us in ordinary life, as well as certain other forms not so well known except to the occultist. The classification of the Seven Minor Mental Planes is more or less satisfactory and arbitrary (unless accompanied by elaborate explanations which are foreign to the purpose of this particular work), but we may as well mention them.

They are as follows:

I. The Plane of Mineral Mind.
II. The Plane of Elemental Mind (A).
III. The Plane of Plant Mind.
IV. The Plane of Elemental Mind (B).
V. The Plane of Animal Mind.
VI. The Plane of Elemental Mind (C).
VII. The Plane of Human Mind.

The Plane of Mineral Mind comprises the "states or conditions" of the units or entities, or groups and combinations of the same, which animate the forms known to us as "minerals, chemicals, etc." These entities must not be confounded with the molecules, atoms and corpuscles themselves, the latter being merely the material bodies or forms of these entities, just as a man's body is but his material form and not "himself." These entities may be called "souls" in one sense, and are living beings of a low degree of development, life, and mind—just a little more than the units of "living energy" which comprise the higher sub-divisions of the highest Physical Plane. The average mind does not generally attribute the possession of mind, soul, or life, to the mineral kingdom, but all occultists recognize the existence of the same, and modern science is rapidly moving forward to the point-of-view of the Hermetic, in this respect. The molecules, atoms and corpuscles have their "loves and hates"; "likes and dislikes"; "attractions and repulsions". "affinities and non-affinities," etc., and some of the more daring of modern scientific minds have expressed the opinion that the desire and will, emotions and feelings, of the atoms differ only in degree from those of men. We have no time or space to argue this matter here. All occultists know it to be a fact, and others are referred to some of the more recent scientific works for outside corroboration. There are the usual seven sub-divisions to this plane.

The Plane of Elemental Mind (A) comprises the state or condition, and degree of mental and vital development of a class of entities unknown to the average man, but recognized to occultists. They are

invisible to the ordinary senses of man, but, nevertheless, exist and play their part of the Drama of the Universe. Their degree of intelligence is between that of the mineral and chemical entities on the one hand, and of the entities of the plant kingdom on the other. There are seven subdivisions to this plane, also.

The Plane of Plant Mind, in its seven sub-divisions, comprises the states or conditions of the entities comprising the kingdoms of the Plant World, the vital and mental phenomena of which is fairly well understood by the average intelligent person, many new and interesting scientific works regarding "Mind and Life in Plants" having been published during the last decade. Plants have life, mind and "souls," as well as have the animals, man, and super-man.

The Plane of Elemental Mind (B), in its seven sub-divisions, comprises the states and conditions of a higher form of "elemental" or unseen entities, playing their part in the general work of the Universe, the mind and life of which form a part of the scale between the Plane of Plant Mind and the Plane of Animal Mind, the entities partaking of the nature of both.

The Plane of Animal Mind, in its seven sub-divisions, comprises the states and conditions of the entities, beings, or souls, animating the animal forms of life, familiar to us all. It is not necessary to go into details regarding this kingdom or plane of life, for the animal world is as familiar to us as is our own.

The Plane of Elemental Mind (C), in its seven sub-divisions, comprises those entities or beings, invisible as are all such elemental forms, which partake of the nature of both animal and human life in a degree and in certain combinations. The highest forms are semi-human in intelligence.

The Plane of Human Mind, in its seven sub-divisions, comprises those manifestations of life and mentality which are common to Man, in his various grades, degrees, and divisions. In this connection, we wish to point out the fact that the average man of today occupies but the fourth sub-division of the Plane of Human Mind, and only the most intelligent have crossed the borders of the Fifth Sub-Division. It has taken the race millions of years to reach this stage, and it will take many more years for the race to move on to the sixth and seventh subdivisions, and beyond. But, remember, that there have been races before us which have passed through these degrees, and then on to higher planes. Our own race is the fifth (with stragglers from the fourth) which has set foot upon The Path. And, then there are a few advanced souls of our own race who have outstripped the masses, and who have passed on to the sixth and seventh sub-division, and some few being still further on. The man of the Sixth Sub-Division will be "The Super Man"; he of the Seventh will be "The Over-Man."

In our consideration of the Seven Minor Mental Planes, we have

merely referred to the Three Elementary Planes in a general way. We do not wish to go into this subject in detail in this work, for it does not belong to this part of the general philosophy and teachings. But we may say this much, in order to give you a little clearer idea. of the relations of these planes to the more familiar ones—the Elementary Planes bear the same relation to the Planes of Mineral, Plant, Animal and Human Mentality and Life, that the black keys on the piano do to the white keys. The white keys are sufficient to produce music, but there are certain scales, melodies, and harmonies, in which the black keys play their part, and in which their presence is necessary. They are also necessary as "connecting links" of soul-condition; entity states, etc., between the several other and in certain combinations. The highest forms are semi-human in intelligence.

The Plane of Human Mind, in its seven sub-divisions, comprises those manifestations of life and mentality which are common to Man, in his various grades, degrees, and divisions. In this connection, we wish to point out the fact that the average man of today occupies but the fourth sub-division of the Plane of Human Mind, and only the most intelligent have crossed the borders of the Fifth Sub-Division. It has taken the race millions of years to reach this stage, and it will take many more years for the race to move on to the sixth and seventh sub-divisions, and beyond. But, remember, that there have been races before us which have passed through these degrees, and then on to higher planes. Our own race is the fifth (with stragglers from the fourth) which has set foot upon The Path. And, then there are a few advanced souls of our own race who have outstripped the masses, and who have passed on to the sixth and seventh sub-division, and some few being still further on. The man of the Sixth Sub-Division will be "The Super Man"; he of the Seventh will be "The Over-Man."

In our consideration of the Seven Minor Mental Planes, we have merely referred to the Three Elementary Planes in a general way. We do not wish to go into this subject in detail in this work, for it does not belong to this part of the general philosophy and teachings. But we may say this much, in order to give you a little clearer idea. of the relations of these planes to the more familiar ones—the Elementary Planes bear the same relation to the Planes of Mineral, Plant, Animal and Human Mentality and Life, that the black keys on the piano do to the white keys. The white keys are sufficient to produce music, but there are certain scales, melodies, and harmonies, in which the black keys play their part, and in which their presence is necessary. They are also necessary as "connecting links" of soul-condition; entity states, etc. between the several other planes, certain forms of development being attained therein—this last fact giving to the reader who can "read between the lines" a new light upon the processes of Evolution, and a new key to the secret door of the "leaps of life" between kingdom and

kingdom. The great kingdoms of Elementals are fully recognized by all occultists, and the esoteric writings are full of mention of them. The readers of Bulwer's "Zanoni" and similar tales will recognize the entities inhabiting these planes of life.

Passing on from the Great Mental Plane to the Great Spiritual Plane, what shall we say? How can we explain these higher states of Being, Life and Mind, to minds as yet unable to grasp and understand the higher sub-divisions of the Plane of Human Mind? The task is impossible. We can speak only in the most general terms. How may Light be described to a man born blind—how sugar, to a man who has never tasted anything sweet—how harmony, to one born deaf?

All that we can say is that the Seven Minor Planes of the Great Spiritual Plane (each Minor Plane having its seven subdivisions) comprise Beings possessing Life, Mind and Form as far above that of man of to-day as the latter is above the earthworm, mineral or even certain forms of Energy or Matter. The Life of these Beings so far transcends ours, that we cannot even think of the details of the same; their minds so far transcend ours, that to them we scarcely seem to "think," and our mental processes seem almost akin to material processes; the Matter of which their forms are composed is of the highest Planes of Matter, nay, some are even said to be "clothed in Pure Energy." What may be said of such Beings?

On the Seven Minor Planes of the Great Spiritual Plane exist Beings of whom we may speak as Angels; Archangels; Demi Gods. On the lower Minor Planes dwell those great souls whom we call Masters and Adepts. Above them come the Great Hierarchies of the Angelic Hosts, unthinkable to man; and above those come those who may without irreverence be called "The Gods," so high in the scale of Being are they, their being, intelligence and power being akin to those attributed by the races of men to their conceptions of Deity. These Beings are beyond even the highest flights of the human imagination, the word "Divine" being the only one applicable to them. Many of these Beings, as well as the Angelic Host, take the greatest interest in the affairs of the Universe and play an important part in its affairs. These Unseen Divinities and Angelic Helpers extend their influence freely and powerfully, in the process of Evolution, and Cosmic Progress. Their occasional intervention and assistance in human affairs have led to the many legends, beliefs, religions and traditions of the race, past and present. They have super-imposed their knowledge and power upon the world, again and again, all under the Law of THE ALL, of course.

But, yet, even the highest of these advanced Beings exist merely as creations of, and in, the Mind of THE ALL, and are subject to the Cosmic Processes and Universal Laws. They are still Mortal. We may call them "gods" if we like, but still. they are but the Elder Brethren of

the Race,—the advanced souls who have outstripped their brethren, and who have foregone the ecstasy of Absorption by THE ALL, in order to help the race on its upward journey along The Path. But, they belong to the Universe, and are subject to its conditions—they are mortal—and their plane is below that of Absolute Spirit.

Only the most advanced Hermetists are able to grasp the Inner Teachings regarding the state of existence, and the powers manifested on the Spiritual Planes. The phenomena is so much higher than that of the Mental Planes that a confusion of ideas would surely result from an attempt to describe the same. Only those whose minds have been carefully trained along the lines of the Hermetic Philosophy for years— yes, those who have brought with them from other incarnations the knowledge acquired previously—can comprehend just what is meant by the Teaching regarding these Spiritual Planes. And much of these Inner Teachings is held by the Hermetists as being too sacred, important and even dangerous for general public dissemination. The intelligent student may recognize what we mean by this when we state that the meaning of "Spirit" as used by the Hermetists is akin to "Living Power"; "Animated Force;" "Inner Essence;" "Essence of Life," etc., which meaning must not be confounded with that usually and commonly employed in connection with the term, i.e., "religious; ecclesiastical; spiritual; ethereal; holy," etc., etc. To occultists the word "Spirit" is used in the sense of "The Animating Principle," carrying with it the idea of Power, Living Energy, Mystic Force, etc. And occultists know that that which is known to them as "Spiritual Power" may be employed for evil as well as good ends (in accordance with the Principle of Polarity), a fact which has been recognized by the majority of religions in their conceptions of Satan, Beelzebub, the Devil, Lucifer, Fallen Angels, etc. And so the knowledge regarding these Planes has been kept in the Holy of Holies in all Esoteric Fraternities and Occult Orders,—in the Secret Chamber of the Temple. But this may be said here, that those who have attained high spiritual powers and have misused them, have a terrible fate in store for them, and the swing of the pendulum of Rhythm will inevitably swing them back to the furthest extreme of Material existence, from which point they must retrace their steps Spiritward, along the weary rounds of The Path, but always with the added torture of having always with them a lingering memory of the heights from which they fell owing to their evil actions. The legends of the Fallen Angels have a basis in actual facts, as all advanced occultists know. The striving for selfish power on the Spiritual Planes inevitably results in the selfish soul losing its spiritual balance and falling back as far as it had previously risen. But to even such a soul, the opportunity of a return is given—and such souls make the return journey, paying the terrible penalty according to the invariable Law.

In conclusion we would again remind you that according to the Principle of Correspondence, which embodies the truth: "As Above so Below; as Below, so Above," all of the Seven Hermetic Principles are in full operation on all of the many planes, Physical Mental and Spiritual. The Principle of Mental Substance of course applies to all the planes, for all are held in the Mind of THE ALL. The Principle of Correspondence manifests in all, for there is a correspondence, harmony and agreement between the several planes. The Principle of Vibration manifests on all planes, in fact the very differences that go to make the "planes" arise from Vibration, as we have explained. The Principle of Polarity manifests on each plane, the extremes of the Poles being apparently opposite and contradictory. The Principle of Rhythm manifests on each Plane, the movement of the phenomena having its ebb and flow, rise and flow, incoming and outgoing. The Principle of Cause and Effect manifests on each Plane, every Effect having its Cause and every Cause having its effect. The Principle of Gender manifests on each Plane, the Creative Energy being always manifest, and operating along the lines of its Masculine and Feminine Aspects.

"As Above so Below; as Below, so Above." This centuries old Hermetic axiom embodies one of the great Principles of Universal Phenomena. As we proceed with our consideration of the remaining Principles, we will see even more clearly the truth of the universal nature of third great Principle of Correspondence.

Chapter IX. Vibration

"Nothing rests; everything moves; everything vibrates."—*The Kybalion.*

The great Third Hermetic Principle—the Principle of Vibration— embodies the truth that Motion is manifest in everything in the Universe—that nothing is at rest—that everything moves, vibrates, and circles. This Hermetic Principle was recognized by some of the early Greek philosophers who embodied it in their systems. But, then, for centuries it was lost sight of by the thinkers outside of the Hermetic ranks. But in the Nineteenth Century physical science re-discovered the truth and the Twentieth Century scientific discoveries have added additional proof of the correctness and truth of this centuries-old Hermetic doctrine. The Hermetic Teachings are that not only is everything in constant movement and vibration, but that the "differences" between the various manifestations of the universal power are due entirely to the varying rate and mode of vibrations. Not only this, but that even THE ALL, in itself, manifests a constant vibration of such an infinite degree of intensity and rapid motion that it may be practically considered as at rest, the teachers directing the attention of the students to the fact that even on the physical plane a rapidly moving object (such as a revolving wheel) seems to be at rest. The Teachings are to the effect that Spirit is at one end of the Pole of Vibration, the other Pole being certain extremely gross forms of Matter. Between these two poles are millions upon millions of different rates and modes of vibration.

Modern Science has proven that all that we call Matter and Energy are but "modes of vibratory motion," and some of the more advanced scientists are rapidly moving toward the positions of the occultists who hold that the phenomena of Mind are likewise modes of vibration or motion. Let us see what science has to say regarding the question of vibrations in matter and energy.

In the first place, science teaches that all matter manifests, in some degree, the vibrations arising from temperature or heat. Be an object cold or hot—both being but degrees of the same things—it manifests certain heat vibrations, and in that sense is. in motion and vibration. Then all particles of Matter are in circular movement, from corpuscle to suns. The planets revolve around suns, and many of them turn on their axes. The suns move around greater central points, and these are believed to move around still greater, and so on, ad infinitum. The molecules of which the particular kinds of Matter are composed are in a state of constant vibration and movement around each other and against each other. The molecules are composed of Atoms, which, likewise, are

in a state of constant movement and vibration. The atoms are composed of Corpuscles, sometimes called "electrons," "ions," etc., which also are in a state of rapid motion, revolving around each other, and which manifest a very rapid state and mode of vibration. And, so we see that all forms of Matter manifest Vibration, in accordance with the Hermetic Principle of Vibration.

And so it is with the various forms of Energy. Science teaches that Light, Heat, Magnetism and Electricity are but forms of vibratory motion connected in some way with, and probably emanating from the Ether. Science does not as yet attempt to explain the nature of the phenomena known as Cohesion, which is the principle of Molecular Attraction; nor Chemical Affinity, which is the principle of Atomic Attraction; nor Gravitation (the greatest mystery of the three), which is the principle of attraction by which every particle or mass of Matter is bound to every other particle or mass. These three forms of Energy are not as yet understood by science, yet the writers incline to the opinion that these too are manifestations of some form of vibratory energy, a fact which the Hermetists have held and taught for ages past.

The Universal Ether, which is postulated by science without its nature being understood clearly, is held by the Hermetists to be but a higher manifestation of that which is erroneously called matter—that is to say, Matter at a higher degree of vibration—and is called by them "The Ethereal Substance." The Hermetists teach that this Ethereal Substance is of extreme tenuity and elasticity, and pervades universal space, serving as a medium of transmission of waves of vibratory energy, such as heat, light, electricity, magnetism, etc. The Teachings are that The Ethereal Substance is a connecting link between the forms of vibratory energy known as "Matter" on the one hand, and "Energy or Force" on the other; and also that it manifests a degree of vibration, in rate and mode, entirely its own.

Scientists have offered the illustration of a rapidly moving wheel, top, or cylinder, to show the effects of increasing rates of vibration. The illustration supposes a wheel, top, or revolving cylinder, running at a low rate of speed—we will call this revolving thing "the object" in following out the illustration. Let us suppose the object moving slowly. It may be seen readily, but no sound of its movement reaches the ear. The speed is gradually increased. In a few moments its movement becomes so rapid that a deep growl or low note may be heard. Then as the rate is increased the note rises one in the musical scale. Then, the motion being still further increased, the next highest note is distinguished. Then, one after another, all the notes of the musical scale appear, rising higher and higher as the motion is increased. Finally when the motions have reached a certain rate the final note perceptible to human ears is reached and the shrill, piercing shriek dies away, and silence follows. No sound is heard from the revolving object, the rate of

motion being so high that the human ear cannot register the vibrations. Then comes the perception of rising degrees of Heat. Then after quite a time the eye catches a glimpse of the object becoming a dull dark reddish color. As the rate increases, the red becomes brighter. Then as the speed is increased, the red melts into an orange. Then the orange melts into a yellow. Then follow, successively, the shades of green, blue, indigo, and finally violet, as the rate of sped increases. Then the violet shades away, and all color disappears, the human eye not being able to register them. But there are invisible rays emanating from the revolving object, the rays that are used in photographing, and other subtle rays of light. Then begin to manifest the peculiar rays known as the "X Rays," etc., as the constitution of the object changes. Electricity and Magnetism are emitted when the appropriate rate of vibration is attained.

When the object reaches a certain rate of vibration its molecules disintegrate, and resolve themselves into the original elements or atoms. Then the atoms, following the Principle of Vibration, are separated into the countless corpuscles of which they are composed. And finally, even the corpuscles disappear and the object may be said to Be composed of The Ethereal Substance. Science does not dare to follow the illustration further, but the Hermetists teach that if the vibrations be continually increased the object would mount up the successive states of manifestation and would in turn manifest the various mental stages, and then on Spiritward, until it would finally re-enter THE ALL, which is Absolute Spirit. The "object," however, would have ceased to be an "object" long before the stage of Ethereal Substance was reached, but otherwise the illustration is correct inasmuch as it shows the effect of constantly increased rates and modes of vibration. It must be remembered, in the above illustration, that at the stages at which the "object" throws off vibrations of light, heat, etc., it is not actually "resolved" into those forms of energy (which are much higher in the scale), but simply that it reaches a degree of vibration in which those forms of energy are liberated, in a degree, from the confining influences of its molecules, atoms and corpuscles, as the case may be. These forms of energy, although much higher in the scale than matter, are imprisoned and confined in the material combinations, by reason of the energies manifesting through, and using material forms, but thus becoming entangled and confined in their creations of material forms, which, to an extent, is true of all creations, the creating force becoming involved in its creation.

But the Hermetic Teachings go much further than do those of modern science. They teach that all manifestation of thought, emotion, reason, will or desire, or any mental state or condition, are accompanied by vibrations, a portion of which are thrown off and which tend to affect the minds of other persons by "induction." This is

the principle which produces the phenomena of "telepathy"; mental influence, and other forms of the action and power of mind over mind, with which the general public is rapidly becoming acquainted, owing to the wide dissemination of occult knowledge by the various schools, cults and teachers along these lines at this time.

Every thought, emotion or mental state has its corresponding rate and mode of vibration. And by an effort of the will of the person, or of other persons, these mental states may be reproduced, just as a musical tone may be reproduced by causing an instrument to vibrate at a certain rate—just as color may be reproduced in the same may. By a knowledge of the Principle of Vibration, as applied to Mental Phenomena, one may polarize his mind at any degree he wishes, thus gaining a perfect control over his mental states, moods, etc. In the same way he may affect the minds of others, producing the desired mental states in them. In short, he may be able to produce on the Mental Plane that which science produces on the Physical Plane—namely, "Vibrations at Will." This power of course may be acquired only by the proper instruction, exercises, practice, etc., the science being that of Mental Transmutation, one of the branches of the Hermetic Art.

A little reflection on what we have said will show the student that the Principle of Vibration underlies the wonderful phenomena of the power manifested by the Masters and Adepts, who are able to apparently set aside the Laws of Nature, but who, in reality, are simply using one law against another; one principle against others; and who accomplish their results by changing the vibrations of material objects, or forms of energy, and thus perform what are commonly called "miracles." As one of the old Hermetic writers has truly said: "He who understands the Principle of Vibration, has grasped the sceptre of Power."

Chapter X. Polarity

"Everything is dual; everything has poles; everything has its pair of opposites; like and unlike are the same; opposites are identical in nature, but different in degree; extremes meet; all truths are but half-truths; all paradoxes may be reconciled."—*The Kybalion.*

The great Fourth Hermetic Principle—the Principle of Polarity embodies the truth that all manifested things have "two sides"; "two aspects"; "two poles"; a "pair of opposites," with manifold degrees between the two extremes. The old paradoxes, which have ever perplexed the mind of men, are explained by an understanding of this Principle. Man has always recognized something akin to this Principle, and has endeavored to express it by such sayings, maxims and aphorisms as the following: "Everything is and isn't, at the same time"; "all truths are but half-truths"; "every truth is half-false"; "there are two sides to everything"—"there is a reverse side to every shield," etc., etc. The Hermetic Teachings are to the effect that the difference between things seemingly diametrically opposed to each other is merely a matter of degree. It teaches that "the pairs of opposites may be reconciled, "and that "thesis and anti-thesis are identical in nature, but different in degree"; and that the "universal reconciliation of opposites" is effected by a recognition of this Principle of Polarity. The teachers claim that illustrations of this Principle may be had on every hand, and from an examination into the real nature of anything. They begin by showing that Spirit and Matter are but the two poles of the same thing, the intermediate planes being merely degrees of vibration. They show that THE ALL and The Many are the same, the difference being merely a matter of degree of Mental Manifestation. Thus the LAW and Laws are the two opposite poles of one thing. Likewise, PRINCIPLE and Principles. Infinite Mind and finite minds.

Then passing on to the Physical Plane, they illustrate the Principle by showing that Heat and Cold are identical in nature, the differences being merely a matter of degrees. The thermometer shows many degrees of temperature, the lowest pole being called "cold," and the highest "heat." Between these two poles are many degrees of "heat" or "cold," call them either and you are equally correct. The higher of two degrees is always "warmer," while the lower is always "colder." There is no absolute standard—all is a matter of degree. There is no place on the thermometer where heat ceases and cold begins. It is all a matter of higher or lower vibrations. The very terms "high" and "low," which we are compelled to use, are but poles of the same thing—the terms are relative. So with "East and West"—travel around the world in an eastward direction, and you reach a point which is called west at your

starting point, and you return from that westward point. Travel far enough North, and you will find yourself traveling South, or vice versa.

Light and Darkness are poles of the same thing, with many degrees between them. The musical scale is the same—starting with "C" you move upward until you reach another "C" and so on, the differences between the two ends of the board being the same, with many degrees between the two extremes. The scale of color is the same—higher and lower vibrations being the only difference between high violet and low red. Large and Small are relative. So are Noise and Quiet; Hard and Soft follow the rule. Likewise Sharp and Dull. Positive and Negative are two poles of the same thing, with countless degrees between them.

Good and Bad are not absolute we call one end of the scale Good and the other Bad, or one end Good and the other Evil, according to the use of the terms. A thing is "less good" than the thing higher in the scale; but that "less good" thing, in turn, is "more good" than the thing next below it—and so on, the "more or less" being regulated by the position on the scale.

And so it is on the Mental Plane. "Love and. Hate" are generally regarded as being things diametrically opposed to each other; entirely different; unreconcilable. But we apply the Principle of Polarity; we find that there is no such thing as Absolute Love or Absolute Hate, as distinguished from each other. The two are merely terms applied to the two poles of the same thing. Beginning at any point of the scale we find "more love," or "less hate," as we ascend the scale; and "more hate" or "less love" as we descend this being true no matter from what point, high or low, we may start. There are degrees of Love and Hate, and there is a middle point where "Like and Dislike" become so faint that it is difficult to distinguish between them. Courage and Fear come under the same rule. The Pairs of Opposites exist everywhere. Where you find one thing you find its opposite—the two poles.

And it is this fact that enables the Hermetist to transmute one mental state into another, along the lines of Polarization. Things belonging to different classes cannot be transmuted into each other, but things of the same class may be changed, that is, may have their polarity changed. Thus Love never becomes East or West, or Red or Violet—but it may and often does turn into Hate and likewise Hate may be transformed into Love, by changing its polarity. Courage may be transmuted into Fear, and the reverse. Hard things may be rendered Soft. Dull things become Sharp. Hot things become Cold. And so on, the transmutation always being between things of the same kind of different degrees. Take the case of a Fearful man. By raising his mental vibrations along the line of Fear-Courage, he can be filled with the highest degree of Courage and Fearlessness. And, likewise, the Slothful man may change himself into an Active, Energetic individual simply by polarizing along the lines of the desired quality.

The student who is familiar with the processes by which the various schools of Mental Science, etc., produce changes in the mental states of those following their teachings, may not readily understand the principle underlying many of these changes. When, however, the Principle of Polarity is once grasped, and it is seen that the mental changes are occasioned by a change of polarity—a sliding along the same scale—the hatter is readily understood. The change is not in the nature of a transmutation of one thing into another thing entirely different—but is merely a change of degree in the same things, a vastly important difference. For instance, borrowing an analogy from the Physical Plane, it is impossible to change Heat into Sharpness, Loudness, Highness, etc., but Heat may readily be transmuted into Cold, simply by lowering the vibrations. In the same way Hate and Love are mutually transmutable; so are Fear and Courage. But Fear cannot be transformed into Love, nor can Courage be transmuted into Hate. The mental states belong to innumerable classes, each class of which has its opposite poles, along which transmutation is possible.

The student will readily recognize that in the mental states, as well as in the phenomena of the Physical Plane, the two poles may be classified as Positive and Negative, respectively. Thus Love is Positive to Hate; Courage to Fear; Activity to Non-Activity, etc., etc. And it will also be noticed that even to those unfamiliar with the Principle of Vibration, the Positive pole seems to be of a higher degree than the Negative, and readily dominates it. The tendency of Nature is in the direction of the dominant activity of the Positive pole.

In addition to the changing of the poles of one's own mental states by the operation of the art of Polarization, the phenomena of Mental Influence, in its manifold phases, shows us that the principle may be extended so as to embrace the phenomena of the influence of one mind over that of another, of which so much has been written and taught of late years. When it is understood that Mental Induction is possible, that is that mental states may be produced by "induction" from others, then we can readily see how a certain rate of vibration, or polarization of a certain mental state, may be communicated to another person, and his polarity in that class of mental states thus changed. It is along this principle that the results of many of the "mental treatments" are obtained. For instance, a person is "blue," melancholy and full of fear. A mental scientist bringing his own mind up to the desired vibration by his trained will, and thus obtaining the desired polarization in his own case, then produces a similar mental state in the other by induction, the result being that the vibrations are raised and the person polarizes toward the Positive end of the scale instead toward the Negative, and his Fear and other negative emotions are transmuted to Courage and similar positive mental states. A little study will show you that these mental changes are nearly all along the line of Polarization, the change

being one of degree rather than of kind.

A knowledge of the existence of this great Hermetic Principle will enable the student to better understand his own mental states, and those of other people. He will see that these states are all matters of degree, and seeing thus, he will be able to raise or lower the vibration at will— to change his mental poles, and thus be Master of his mental states, instead of being their servant and slave. And by his knowledge he will be able to aid his fellows intelligently and by the appropriate methods change the polarity when the same is desirable. We advise all students to familiarize themselves with this Principle of Polarity, for a correct understanding of the same will throw light on many difficult subjects.

Chapter XI. Rhythm

"Everything flows out and in; everything has its tides; all things rise and fall; the pendulum-swing manifests in everything; the measure of the swing to the right, is the measure of the swing to the left; rhythm compensates"—*The Kybalion.*

The great Fifth Hermetic Principle—the Principle of Rhythm—embodies the truth that in everything there is manifested a measured motion; a to-and-from movement; a flow and inflow; a swing forward and backward; a pendulum-like movement; a tide-like ebb and flow; a high-tide and a low-tide; between the two—poles manifest on the physical, mental or spiritual planes. The Principle of rhythm is closely connected with the Principle of Polarity described in the preceding chapter. Rhythm manifests between the two poles established by the Principle of Polarity. This does not mean, however, that the pendulum of Rhythm swings to the extreme poles, for this rarely happens; in fact, it is difficult to establish the extreme polar opposites in the majority of cases. But the swing is ever "toward" first one pole and then the other.

There is always an action and reaction; an advance and a retreat; a rising and sinking; manifested in all of the airs and phenomena of the Universe. Suns, worlds, men, animals, plants, minerals, forces, energy, mind and matter, yes, even Spirit, manifests this Principle. The Principle manifests in the creation and destruction of worlds; in the rise and fall of nations in the life history of all things; and finally in the mental states of Man.

Beginning with the manifestations of Spirit—of THE ALL—it will be noticed that there is ever the Outpouring and the Indrawing; the "Outbreathing and Inbreathing of Brahm," as the Brahmans word it. Universes are created; reach their extreme low point of materiality; and then begin in their upward swing. Suns spring into being, and then their height of power being reached, the process of retrogression begins, and after aeons they become dead masses of matter, awaiting another impulse which starts again their inner energies into activity and a new solar life cycle is begun. And thus it is with all the worlds; they are born, grow and die; only to be reborn. And thus it is with all the things of shape and form; they swing from action to reaction; from birth to death; from activity to inactivity—and then back again. Thus it is with all living things they are born, grow, and die—and then are reborn. So it is with all great movements, philosophies, creeds, fashions, governments, nations, and all else—birth, growth, maturity, decadence, death—and then new birth. The swing of the pendulum is ever in evidence.

Night follows day; and day night. The pendulum swings from

Summer to Winter, and then back again. The corpuscles, atoms, molecules, and all masses of matter, swing around the circle of their nature. There is no such thing as absolute rest, or cessation from movement, and all movement partakes of rhythm. The Principle is of universal application. It may be applied to any question, or phenomena of any of the many planes of life. It may be applied to all phases of human activity.

There is always the Rhythmic swing from one pole to the other. The Universal Pendulum is ever in motion. The Tides of Life flow in and out, according to Law.

The Principle of rhythm is well understood by modern science, and is considered a universal law as applied to material things. But the Hermetists carry the principle much further, and know that its manifestations and influence extend to the mental activities of Man, and that it accounts for the bewildering succession of moods, feelings and other annoying and perplexing changes that we notice in ourselves. But the Hermetists by studying the operations of this Principle have learned to escape some of its activities by Transmutation.

The Hermetic Masters long since discovered that while the Principle of Rhythm was invariable, and ever in evidence in mental phenomena, still there were two planes of its manifestation so far as mental phenomena are concerned. They discovered that there were two general planes of Consciousness, the Lower and the Higher, the understanding of which fact enabled them to rise to the higher plane and thus escape the swing of the Rhythmic pendulum which manifested on the lower plane. In other words, the swing of the pendulum occurred on the Unconscious Plane, and the Consciousness was not affected. This they call the Law of Neutralization. Its operations consist in the raising of the Ego above the vibrations of the Unconscious Plane of mental activity, so that the negative-swing of the pendulum is not manifested in consciousness, and therefore they are not affected. It is akin to rising above a thing and letting it pass beneath you. The Hermetic Master, or advanced student, polarizes himself at the desired pole, and by a process akin to "refusing" to participate in the backward swing or, if you prefer, a "denial" of its influence over him, he stands firm in his polarized position, and allows the mental pendulum to swing back along the unconscious plane. All individuals who have attained any degree of self-mastery, accomplish this, more or less unknowingly, and by refusing to allow their moods and negative mental states to affect them, they apply the Law of Neutralization. The Master, however, carries this to a much higher degree of proficiency, and by the use of his Will he attains a degree of Poise and Mental Firmness almost impossible of belief on the part of those who allow themselves to be swung backward and forward by the mental pendulum of moods and feelings.

The importance of this will be appreciated by any thinking person who realizes what creatures of moods, feelings and emotion the majority of people are, and how little mastery of themselves they manifest. If you will stop and consider a moment, you will realize how much these swings of Rhythm have affected you in your life—how a period of Enthusiasm has been invariably followed by an opposite feeling and mood of Depression. Likewise, your moods and periods of Courage have been succeeded by equal moods of Fear. And so it has ever been with the majority of persons—tides of feeling have ever risen and fallen with them, but they have never suspected the cause or reason of the mental phenomena. An understanding of the workings of this Principle will give one the key to the Mastery of these rhythmic swings of feeling, and will enable him to know himself better and to avoid being carried away by these inflows and outflows. The Will is superior to the conscious manifestation of this Principle, although the Principle itself can never be destroyed. We may escape its effects, but the Principle operates, nevertheless. The pendulum ever swings, although we may escape being carried along with it.

There are other features of the operation of this Principle of Rhythm of which we wish to speak at this point. There comes into its operations that which is known as the Law of Compensation. One of the definitions or meanings of the word "Compensate" is, "to counterbalance" which is the sense in which the Hermetists use the term. It is this Law of Compensation to which the Kybalion refers when it says: " The measure of the swing to the right is the measure of the swing to the left; rhythm, compensates."

The Law of Compensation is that the swing in one direction determines the swing in the opposite direction, or to the opposite pole—the one balances, or counterbalances, the other. On the Physical Plane we see many examples of this Law. The pendulum of the clock swings a certain distance to the right, and then an equal distance to the left. The seasons balance each other in the same way. The tides follow the same Law. And the same Law is manifested in all the phenomena of Rhythm. The pendulum, with a short swing in one direction, has but a short swing—in the other; while the long swing to the right invariably means the long swing to the left.

An object hurled upward to a certain height has an equal distance to traverse on its return. The force with which a projectile is sent upward a mile is reproduced when the projectile returns to the earth on its return journey. This Law is constant on the Physical Plane, as reference to the standard authorities will show you.

But the Hermetists carry it still further. They teach that a man's mental states are subject to the same Law. The man who enjoys keenly, is subject to keen suffering; while he who feels but little pain is capable of feeling but little joy. The pig suffers but little mentally, and enjoys

but little—he is compensated. And on the other hand, there are other animals who enjoy keenly, but whose nervous organism and temperament cause them to suffer exquisite degrees of pain and so it is with Man. There are temperaments which permit of but low degrees of enjoyment, and equally low degrees of suffering; while there are others which permit the most intense enjoyment, but also the most intense suffering. The rule is that the capacity for pain and pleasure, in each individual, are balanced. The Law of Compensation is in full operation here. But the Hermetists go still further in this matter. They teach that before one is able to enjoy a certain degree of pleasure, he must have swung as far, proportionately, toward the other pole of feeling. They hold, however, that the Negative is precedent to the Positive in this matter, that is to say that in experiencing a certain degree of pleasure it does not follow that he will have to "pay up for it" with a corresponding degree of pain; on the contrary, the pleasure is the Rhythmic swing, according to the Law of Compensation, for a degree of pain previously experienced either in the present life, or in a previous incarnation. This throws a new light on the Problem of Pain.

The Hermetists regard the chain of lives as continuous, and as forming a part of one life of the individual, so that in consequence the rhythmic swing is understood in this way, while it would be without meaning unless the truth of reincarnation is admitted.

But the Hermetists claim that the Master or advanced student is able, to a great degree, to escape the swing toward Pain, by the process of Neutralization before mentioned. By rising on to the higher plane of the Ego, much of the experience that comes to those dwelling on the lower plane is avoided and escaped.

The Law of Compensation plays an important part in the lives of men and women. It will be noticed that one generally "pays the price" of anything he possesses or lacks. If he has one thing, he lacks another—the balance is struck. No one can "keep his penny and have the bit of cake" at the same time Everything has its pleasant and unpleasant sides. The things that one gains are always paid for by the things that one loses. The rich possess much that the poor lack, while the poor often possess things that are beyond the reach of the rich. The millionaire may have the inclination toward feasting, and the wealth wherewith to secure all the dainties and luxuries of the table, while he lacks the appetite to enjoy the same; he envies the appetite and digestion of the laborer who lacks the wealth and inclinations of the millionaire, and who gets more pleasure from his plain food than the millionaire could obtain even if his appetite were not jaded, nor his digestion ruined, for the wants, habits and inclinations differ. And so it is through life. The Law of Compensation is ever in operation, striving to balance and counter-balance, and always succeeding in time, even though several lives may be required for the return swing of the

Pendulum of Rhythm.

Chapter XII. Causation

"Every Cause has its Effect; every Effect has its Cause; everything happens according to Law; Chance is but a name for Law not recognized; there are many planes of causation, but nothing escapes the Law."—*The Kybalion.*

The great Sixth Hermetic Principle—the Principle of Cause and Effect—embodies the truth that Law pervades the Universe; that nothing happens by Chance that Chance is merely a term indicating cause existing but not recognized or perceived that phenomena is continuous, without break or exception.

The Principle of Cause and Effect underlies all scientific thought, ancient and modern, and was enunciated by the Hermetic Teachers in the earliest days. While many and varied disputes between the many schools of thought have since arisen, these disputes have been principally upon the details of the operations of the Principle, and still more often upon the meaning of certain words. The underlying Principle of Cause and Effect has been accepted as correct by practically all the thinkers of the world worthy of the name. To think otherwise would be to take the phenomena of the universe from the domain of Law and Order, and to relegate it; to the control of the imaginary something which men have called "Chance."

A little consideration will show anyone that there is in reality no such thing as pure chance. Webster defines the word "Chance" as follows: "A supposed agent or mode of activity other than a force, law or purpose; the operation or activity of such agent; the supposed effect of such an agent; a happening; fortuity; casualty, etc." But a little consideration will show you that there can be no such agent as "Chance," in the sense of something outside of Law—something outside of Cause and Effect. How could there be a something acting in the phenomenal universe, independent of the laws, order, and continuity of the latter? Such a something would be entirely independent of the orderly trend of the universe, and therefore superior to it. We can imagine nothing outside of THE ALL being outside of the Law, and that only because THE ALL is the LAW in itself. There is no room in the universe for a something outside of and independent of Law. The existence of such a Something would render all Natural Laws ineffective, and would plunge the universe into chaotic disorder and lawlessness. A careful examination will show that what we call "Chance" is merely an expression relating to obscure causes; causes that we cannot perceive; causes that we cannot understand. The word Chance is derived from a word Meaning "to fall" (as the falling of dice), the idea being that the fall of the dice (and many other

happenings) are merely a "happening" unrelated to any cause. And this is the sense in which the term is generally employed. But when the matter is closely examined, it is seen that there is no chance whatsoever about the fall of the dice. Each time a die falls, and displays a certain number, it obeys a law as infallible as that which governs the revolution of the planets around the sun. Back of the fall of the die are causes, or chains of causes, running back further than the mind can follow. The position of the die in the box; the amount of muscular energy expended in the throw; the condition of the table, etc., etc., all are causes, the effect of which may be seen. But back of these seen causes there are chains of unseen preceding causes, all of which had a bearing upon the number of the die which fell uppermost.

If a die be cast a great number of times, it will be found that the numbers shown will be about equal, that is, there will be an equal number of one-spot, two-spot, etc., coming uppermost. Toss a penny in the air, and it may come down either "heads" or "tails"; but make a sufficient number of tosses, and the heads and tails will about even up. This is the operation of the law of average. But both the average and the single toss come under the Law of Cause and Effect, and if we were able to examine into the preceding causes, it would be clearly seen that it was simply impossible for the die to fall other than it did, under the same circumstances and at the same time. Given the same causes, the same results will follow. There is always a "cause" and a "because" to every event. Nothing ever "happens" without a cause, or rather a chain of causes.

Some confusion has arisen in the minds of persons considering this Principle, from the fact that they were unable to explain how one thing could cause another thing—that is, be the "creator" of the second thing. As a matter of fact, no "thing" ever causes or "creates" another "thing." Cause and Effect deals merely with "events." An "event" is that which comes, arrives or happens, as a result or consequent of some preceding event. No event "creates" another event, but is merely a preceding link in the great orderly chain of events flowing from the creative energy of THE ALL. There is a continuity between all events precedent, consequent and subsequent. There is a relation existing between everything that has gone before, and everything that follows. A stone is dislodged from a mountain side and crashes through a roof of a cottage in the valley below. At first sight we regard this as a chance effect, but when we examine the matter we find a great chain of causes behind it. In the first place there was the rain which softened the earth supporting the stone and which allowed it to fall; then back of that was the influence of the sun, other rains, etc., which gradually disintegrated the piece of rock from a larger piece; then there were the causes which led to the formation of the mountain, and its upheaval by convulsions of nature, and so on ad infinitum. Then we might follow up the causes

behind the rain, etc. Then we might consider the existence of the roof In short, we would soon find ourselves involved in a mesh of cause and effect, from which we would soon strive to extricate ourselves.

Just as a man has two parents, and four grandparents, and eight great-grandparents, and sixteen great-great-grandparents, and so on until when, say, forty generations are calculated the numbers of ancestors run into many millions—so it is with the number of causes behind even the most trifling event or phenomena, such as the passage of a tiny speck of soot before your eye. It is not an easy matter to trace the bit of soot hack to the early period of the world's history when it formed a part of a massive tree-trunk, which was afterward converted into coal, and so on, until as the speck of soot it now passes before your vision on its way to other adventures. And a mighty chain of events, causes and effects, brought it to its present condition, and the later is but one of the chain of events which will go to produce other events hundreds of years from now. One of the series of events arising from the tiny bit of soot was the writing of these lines, which caused the typesetter to perform certain work; the proofreader to do likewise ; and which will arouse certain thoughts in your mind, and that of others, which in turn will affect others, and so on, and on, and on, beyond the ability of man to think further—and all from the passage of a tiny bit of soot, all of which shows the relativity and association of things, and the further fact that "there is no great; there is no small, in the mind that causeth all."

Stop to think a moment. If a certain man had not met a certain maid, away back in the dim period of the Stone Age you who are now reading these lines would not now be here. And if, perhaps, the same couple had failed to meet, we who now write these lines would not now be here. And the very act of writing, on our part, and the act of reading, on yours, will affect not only the respective lives of yourself and ourselves, but will also have a direct, or indirect, affect upon many other people now living and who will live in the ages to come. Every thought we think, every act we perform, has its direct and indirect results which fit into the great chain of Cause and Effect.

We do not wish to enter into a consideration of Free Will, or Determinism, in this work, for various reasons. Among the many reasons, is the principal one that neither side of the controversy is entirely right—in fact, both sides are partially right, according to the Hermetic Teachings. The Principle of Polarity shows that both are but Half-Truths the opposing poles of Truth. The Teachings are that a man may be both Free and yet bound by Necessity, depending upon the meaning of the terms, and the height of Truth from which the matter is examined. The ancient writers express the matter thus: "The further the creation is from the Centre, the more it is bound; the nearer the Centre it reaches, the nearer Free is it."

The majority of people are more or less the slaves of heredity, environment, etc., and manifest very little Freedom. They are swayed by the opinions, customs and thoughts of the outside world, and also by their emotions, feelings, moods, etc. They manifest no Mastery, worthy of the name. They indignantly repudiate this assertion, saying, "Why, I certainly am free to act and do as I please—I do just what I want to do," but they fail to explain whence arise the "want to" and "as I please." What makes them "want to" do one thing in preference to another; what makes them "please" to do this, and not do that? Is there no "because" to their "pleasing" and "Wanting"? The Master can change these "pleases" and "wants" into others at the opposite end of the mental pole. He is able to "Will to will," instead of to will because some feeling, mood, emotion, or environmental suggestion arouses a tendency or desire within him so to do.

The majority of people are carried along like the falling stone, obedient to environment, outside influences and internal moods, desires, etc., not to speak of the desires and wills of others stronger than themselves, heredity, environment, and suggestion, carrying them along without resistance on their part, or the exercise of the Will. Moved like the pawns on the checkerboard of life, they play their parts and are laid aside after the game is over. But the Masters, knowing the rules of the game, rise above the plane of material life, and placing themselves in touch with the higher powers of their nature, dominate their own moods, characters, qualities, and polarity, as well as the environment surrounding them and thus become Movers in the game, instead of Pawns—Causes instead of Effects. The Masters do not escape the Causation of the higher planes, but fall in with the higher laws, and thus master circumstances on the lower plane. They thus form a conscious part of the Law, instead of being mere blind instruments. While they Serve on the Higher Planes, they Rule on the Material Plane.

But, on higher and on lower, the Law is always in operation. There is no such thing as Chance. The blind goddess has been abolished by Reason. We are able to see now, with eyes made clear by knowledge, that everything is governed by Universal Law—that the infinite number of laws are but manifestations of the One Great Law—the LAW which is THE ALL. It is true indeed that not a sparrow drops unnoticed by the Mind of THE ALL that even the hairs on our head are numbered—as the scriptures have said There is nothing outside of Law; nothing that happens contrary to it. And yet, do not make the mistake of supposing that Man is but a blind automaton—far from that. The Hermetic Teachings are that Man may use Law to overcome laws, and that the higher will always prevail against the lower, until at last he has reached the stage in which he seeks refuge in the LAW itself, and laughs the phenomenal laws to scorn. Are you able to grasp the inner meaning of this?

Chapter XIII. Gender

"Gender is in everything; everything has its Masculine and Feminine Principles; Gender manifests on all planes."—*The Kybalion.*

The great Seventh Hermetic Principle—the Principle of Gender—embodies the truth that there is Gender manifested in everything—that the Masculine and Feminine principles are ever present and active in all phases of phenomena, on each and every plane of life. At this point we think it well to call your attention to the fact that Gender, in its Hermetic sense, and Sex in the ordinarily accepted use of the term, are not the same.

The word "Gender" is derived from the Latin root meaning "to beget; to procreate; to generate; to create; to produce." A moment's consideration will show you that the word has a much broader and more general meaning than the term "Sex," the latter referring to the physical distinctions between male and female living things. Sex is merely a manifestation of Gender on a certain plane of the Great Physical Plane—the plane of organic life. We wish to impress this distinction upon your minds, for the reason that certain writers, who have acquired a smattering of the Hermetic Philosophy, have sought to identify this Seventh Hermetic Principle with wild and fanciful, and often reprehensible, theories and teachings regarding Sex.

The office of Gender is solely that of creating, producing, generating, etc., and its manifestations are visible on every plane of phenomena. It is somewhat difficult to produce proofs of this along scientific lines, for the reason that science has not as yet recognized this Principle as of universal application. But still some proofs are forthcoming from scientific sources. In the first place, we find a distinct manifestation of the Principle of Gender among the corpuscles, ions, or electrons, which constitute the basis of Matter as science now knows the latter, and which by forming certain combinations form the Atom, which until lately was regarded as final and indivisible.

The latest word of science is that the atom is composed of a multitude of corpuscles, electrons, or ions (the various names being applied by different authorities) revolving around each other and vibrating at a high degree and intensity. But the accompanying statement is made that the formation of the atom is really due to the clustering of negative corpuscles around a positive one—the positive corpuscles seeming to exert a certain influence upon the negative corpuscles, causing the latter to assume certain combinations and thus "create" or "generate" an atom. This is in line with the most ancient Hermetic Teachings, which have always identified the Masculine principle of Gender with the "Positive," and the Feminine with the

"Negative" Poles of Electricity (so called).

Now a word at this point regarding this identification. The public mind has formed an entirely erroneous impression regarding the qualities of the so-called "Negative" pole of electrified or magnetized Matter. The terms Positive and Negative are very wrongly applied to this phenomenon by science. The word Positive means something real and strong, as compared with a Negative unreality or weakness. Nothing is further from the real facts of electrical phenomenon. The so-called Negative pole of the battery is really the pole in and by which the generation or production of new forms and energies is manifested. There is nothing "negative" about it. The best scientific authorities now use the word "Cathode" in place of "Negative," the word Cathode coming from the Greek root meaning "descent; the path of generation, etc," From the Cathode pole emerge the swarm of electrons or corpuscles; from the same pole emerge those wonderful "rays" which have revolutionized scientific conceptions during the past decade. The Cathode pole is the Mother of all of the strange phenomena which have rendered useless the old text-books, and which have caused many long accepted theories to be relegated to the scrap-pile of scientific speculation. The Cathode, or Negative Pole, is the Mother Principle of Electrical Phenomena, and of the finest forms of matter as yet known to science. So you see we are justified in refusing to use the term "Negative" in our consideration of the subject, and in insisting upon substituting the word "Feminine" for the old term. The facts of the case bear us out in this, without taking the Hermetic Teachings into consideration. And so we shall use the word "Feminine" in the place of "Negative" in speaking of that pole of activity.

The latest scientific teachings are that the creative corpuscles or electrons are Feminine (science says "they are composed of negative electricity"—we say they are composed of Feminine energy). A Feminine corpuscle becomes detached from, or rather leaves, a Masculine corpuscle, and starts on a new career. It actively seeks a union with a Masculine corpuscle, being urged thereto by the natural impulse to create new forms of Matter or Energy. One writer goes so far as to use the term "it at once seeks, of its own volition, a union, " etc. This detachment and uniting form the basis of the greater part of the activities of the chemical world. When the Feminine corpuscle unites with a Masculine corpuscle, a certain process is begun. The Feminine particles vibrate rapidly under the influence of the Masculine energy, and circle rapidly around the latter. The result is the birth of a new atom. This new atom is really composed of a union of the Masculine and Feminine electrons, or corpuscles, but when the union is formed the atom is a separate thing, having certain properties, but no longer manifesting the property of free electricity. The process of detachment or separation of the Feminine electrons is called

"ionization." These electrons, or corpuscles, are the most active workers in Nature's field. Arising from their unions, or combinations, manifest the varied phenomena of light, heat, electricity, magnetism, attraction, repulsion, chemical affinity and the reverse, and similar phenomena. And all this arises from the operation of the Principle of Gender on the plane of Energy.

The part of the Masculine principle seems to be that of directing a certain inherent energy toward the Feminine principle, and thus starting into activity the creative processes. But the Feminine principle is the one always doing the active creative work—and this is so on all planes. And yet, each principle is incapable of operative energy without the assistance of the other. In some of the forms of life, the two principles are combined in one organism. For that matter, everything in the organic world manifests both genders—there is always the Masculine present in the Feminine form, and the Feminine present in the Masculine form. The Hermetic Teachings include much regarding the operation of the two principles of Gender in the production and manifestation of various forms of energy, etc., but we do not deem it expedient to go into detail regarding the same at this point, because we are unable to back up the same with scientific proof, for the reason that science has not as yet progressed thus far. But the example we have given you of the phenomena of the electrons or corpuscles will show you that science is on the right path, and will also give you a general idea of the underlying principles.

Some leading scientific investigators have announced their belief that in the formation of crystals there was to be found something that corresponded to "sex activity" which is another straw showing the direction the scientific winds are blowing. And each year will bring other facts to corroborate the correctness of the Hermetic Principle of Gender. It will be found that Gender is in constant operation and manifestation in the field of inorganic matter, and in the field of Energy or Force. Electricity is now generally regarded as the "Something" into which all other forms of energy seem to melt or dissolve. The "Electrical Theory of the Universe" is the latest scientific doctrine, and is growing rapidly in popularity and general acceptance. And it thus follows that if we are able to discover in the phenomena of electricity—even at the very root and source of its manifestations a clear and unmistakable evidence of the presence of Gender and its activities, we are justified in asking you to believe that science at last has offered proofs of the existence in all universal phenomena of that great Hermetic Principle—the Principle of Gender.

It is not necessary to take up your time with the well known phenomena of the "attraction and repulsion" of the atoms; chemical affinity; the "loves and hates" of the atomic particles; the attraction or cohesion between the molecules of matter. These facts are too well

known to need extended comment from us. But, have you ever considered that all of these things are manifestations of the Gender Principle? Can you not see that the phenomena is "on all fours" with that of the corpuscles or electrons? And more than this, can you not see the reasonableness of the Hermetic Teachings which assert that the very Law of Gravitation—that strange attraction by reason of which all particles and bodies of matter in the universe tend toward each other is but another manifestation of the Principle of Gender, which operates in the direction of attracting the Masculine to the Feminine energies, and vice versa? We cannot offer you scientific proof of this at this time— but examine the phenomena in the light of the Hermetic Teachings on the subject, and see if you have not a better working hypothesis than any offered by physical science. Submit all physical phenomena to the test, and you will discern the Principle of Gender ever in evidence.

Let us now pass on to a consideration of the operation of the Principle on the Mental Plane. Many interesting features are there awaiting examination.

Chapter XIV. Mental Gender

Students of psychology who have followed the modern trend of thought along the lines of mental phenomena are struck by the persistence of the dual-mind idea which has manifested itself so strongly during the past ten or fifteen years, and which has given rise to a number of plausible theories regarding the nature and constitution of these "two minds." The late Thomson J. Hudson attained great popularity in 1893 by advancing his well-known theory of the "objective and subjective minds" which he held existed in every individual. Other writers have attracted almost equal attention by the theories regarding the "conscious and sub-conscious minds"; the "voluntary and involuntary minds"; "the active and passive minds," etc., etc. The theories of the various writers differ from each other, but there remains the underlying principle of "the duality of mind."

The student of the Hermetic Philosophy is tempted to smile when he reads and hears of these many "new theories" regarding the duality of mind, each school adhering tenaciously to its own pet theories, and each claiming to have "discovered the truth." The student turns back the pages of occult history, and away back in the dim beginnings of occult teachings he finds references to the ancient Hermetic doctrine of the Principle of Gender on the Mental Plane—the manifestation of Mental Gender. And examining further he finds that the ancient philosophy took cognizance of the phenomenon of the "dual mind," and accounted for it by the theory of Mental Gender. This idea of Mental Gender may be explained in a few words to students who are familiar with the modern theories just alluded to. The Masculine Principle of Mind corresponds to the so-called Objective Mind; Conscious Mind; Voluntary Mind; Active Mind, etc. And the Feminine Principle of Mind corresponds to the so-called Subjective Mind; Sub-conscious Mind; Involuntary Mind; Passive Mind, etc. Of course the Hermetic Teachings do not agree with the many modern theories regarding the nature of the two phases of mind, nor does it admit many of the facts claimed for the two respective aspects—some of the said theories and claims being very far-fetched and incapable of standing the test of experiment and demonstration.

We point to the phases of agreement merely for the purpose of helping the student to assimilate his previously acquired knowledge with the teachings of the Hermetic Philosophy. Students of Hudson will notice the statement at the beginning of his second chapter of: The Law of Psychic Phenomena," that: "The mystic jargon of the Hermetic philosophers discloses the same general idea"—i.e., the duality of mind. If Dr. Hudson had taken the time and trouble to decipher a little of "the mystic jargon of the Hermetic Philosophy," he might have

received much light upon the subject of "the dual mind"—but then, perhaps, his most interesting work might not have been written. Let us now consider the Hermetic Teachings regarding Mental Gender.

The Hermetic Teachers impart their instruction regarding this subject by bidding their students examine the report of their consciousness regarding their Self. The students are bidden to turn their attention inward upon the Self dwelling within each. Each student is led to see that his consciousness gives him first a report of the existence of his Self—the report is "I Am." This at first seems to be the final words from the consciousness, but a little further examination discloses the fact that this "I Am" may be separated or split into two distinct parts, or aspects, which while working in unison and in conjunction, yet, nevertheless, may be separated in consciousness.

While at first there seems to be only an "I" existing, a more careful and closer examination reveals the fact that there exists an "I" and a "Me." These mental twins differ in their characteristics and nature, and an examination of their nature and the phenomena arising from the same will throw much light upon many of the problems of mental influence.

Let us begin with a consideration of the Me, which is usually mistaken for the I by the student, until he presses the inquiry a little further back into the recesses of consciousness. A man thinks of his Self (in its aspect of Me) as being composed of certain feelings, tastes likes, dislikes, habits, peculiar ties, characteristics, etc., all of which go to make up his personality, or the "Self" known to himself and others. He knows that these emotions and feelings change; are born and die away; are subject to the Principle of Rhythm, and the Principle of Polarity, which take him from one extreme of feeling to another. He also thinks of the "Me" as being certain knowledge gathered together in his mind, and thus forming a part of himself. This is the "Me" of a man.

But we have proceeded too hastily. The "Me" of many men may be said to consist largely of their consciousness of the body and their physical appetites, etc. Their consciousness being largely bound up with their bodily nature, they practically "live there." Some men even go so far as to regard their personal apparel as a part of their "Me" and actually seem to consider it a part of themselves. A writer has humorously said that "men consist of three parts—soul, body and clothes." These "clothes conscious" people would lose their personality if divested of their clothing by savages upon the occasion of a shipwreck. But even many who are not so closely bound up with the idea of personal raiment stick closely to the consciousness of their bodies being their "Me" They cannot conceive of a Self independent of the body. Their mind seems to them to be practically "a something belonging to" their body—which in many cases it is indeed.

But as man rises in the scale of consciousness he is able to

disentangle his "Me" from his idea of body, and is able to think of his body as "belonging to" the mental part of him. But even then he is very apt to identify the "Me" entirely with the mental states, feelings, etc., Which he feels to exist within him. He is very apt to consider these internal states as identical with himself, instead of their being simply "things" produced by some part of his mentality, and existing within him—of him, and in him, but still not "himself." He sees that he may change these internal states of feelings by all effort of will, and that he may produce a feeling or state of an exactly opposite nature, in the same way, and yet the same "Me" exists. And so after a while he is able to set aside these various mental states, emotions, feelings, habits, qualities, characteristics, and other personal mental belongings—he is able to set them aside in the "not-me" collection of curiosities and encumbrances, as well as valuable possessions. This requires much mental concentration and power of mental analysis on the part of the student. But still the task is possible for the advanced student, and even those not so far advanced are able to see, in the imagination, how the process may be performed.

After this laying-aside process has been performed, the student will find himself in conscious possession of a "Self" which may be considered in its "I" and "Me" dual aspects. The "Me" will be felt to be a Something mental in which thoughts, ideas, emotions, feelings, and other mental states may be produced. It may be considered as the "mental womb," as the ancients styled it—capable of generating mental offspring. It reports to the consciousness as a "Me" with latent powers of creation and generation of mental progeny of all sorts and kinds. Its powers of creative energy are felt to be enormous. But still it seems to be conscious that it must receive some form of energy from either its "I" companion, or else from some other "I" ere it is able to bring into being its mental creations. This consciousness brings with it a realization of an enormous capacity for mental work and creative ability.

But the student soon finds that this is not all that he finds within his inner consciousness. He finds that there exists a mental Something which is able to Will that the "Me" act along certain creative lines, and which is also able to stand aside and witness the mental creation. This part of himself he is taught to call his "I." He is able to rest in its consciousness at will. He finds there not a consciousness of an ability to generate and actively create, in the sense of the gradual process attendant upon mental operations, but rather a sense and consciousness of an ability to project an energy from the "I" to the "Me"—a process of "willing" that the mental creation begin and proceed. He also finds that the "I" is able to stand aside and witness the operations of the "Me's" mental creation and generation. There is this dual aspect in the mind of every person. The "I" represents the Masculine Principle of

Mental Gender—the "Me" represents the Female Principle. The "I" represents the Aspect of Being; the "Me" the Aspect of Becoming. You will notice that the Principle of Correspondence operates on this plane just as it does upon the great plane upon which the creation of Universes is performed. The two are similar in kind, although vastly different in degree. "As above, so below; as below, so above."

These aspects of mind—the Masculine and Feminine Principles— the "I" and the "Me"—considered in connection with the well-known mental and psychic phenomena, give the master-key to these dimly known regions of mental operation and manifestation. The principle of Mental Gender gives the truth underlying the whole field of the phenomena of mental influence, etc.

The tendency of the Feminine Principle is always in the direction of receiving impressions, while the tendency of the Masculine Principle is always in the direction of giving, out or expressing. The Feminine Principle has much more varied field of operation than has the Masculine Principle. The Feminine Principle conducts the work of generating new thoughts, concepts, ideas, including the work of the imagination. The Masculine Principle contents itself with the work of the "Will" in its varied phases. And yet, without the active aid of the Will of the Masculine Principle, the Feminine Principle is apt to rest content with generating mental images which are the result of impressions received from outside, Instead of producing original mental creations.

Persons who can give continued attention and thought to a subject actively employ both of the Mental Principles—the Feminine in the work of the mental generation, and the Masculine Will in stimulating and energizing the creative portion of the mind. The majority of persons really employ the Masculine Principle but little, and are content to live according to the thoughts and ideas instilled into the "Me" from the "I" of other minds. But it is not our purpose to dwell upon this phase of the subject, which may be studied from any good text-book upon psychology, with the key that we have given you regarding Mental Gender.

The student of Psychic Phenomena is aware of the wonderful phenomena classified under the head of Telepathy; Thought Transference; Mental Influence; Suggestion; Hypnotism, etc. Many have sought for an explanation of these varied phases of phenomena under the theories of the various "dual mind" teachers. And in a measure they are right, for there is clearly a manifestation of two distinct phases of mental activity. But if such students will consider these "dual minds" in the light of the Hermetic Teachings regarding Vibrations and Mental Gender, they will see that the long sought for key is at hand. In the phenomena of Telepathy it is seen how the Vibratory Energy of the Masculine Principle is projected toward the

Feminine Principle of another person, and the latter takes the seed-thought and allows it to develop into maturity. In the same way Suggestion and Hypnotism operates. The Masculine Principle of the person giving the suggestions directs a stream of Vibratory Energy or Will-Power toward the Feminine Principle of the other person, and the latter accepting it makes it its own and acts and thinks accordingly. An idea thus lodged in the mind of another person grows and develops, and in time is regarded as the rightful mental offspring of the individual, whereas it is in reality like the cuckoo egg placed in the sparrows nest, where it destroys the rightful offspring and makes itself at home. The normal method is for the Masculine and Feminine Principles in a person's mind to co-ordinate and act harmoniously in conjunction with each other, but, unfortunately, the Masculine Principle in the average person is too lazy to act—the display of Will-Power is too slight—and the consequence is that such persons are ruled almost entirely by the minds and wills of other persons, whom they allow to do their thinking and willing for them. How few original thoughts or original actions are performed by the average person? Are not the majority of persons mere shadows and echoes of others having stronger wills or minds than themselves? The trouble is that the average person dwells almost altogether in his "Me" consciousness and does not realize that he has such a thing as an "I." He is polarized in his Feminine Principle of Mind, and the Masculine Principle, in which is lodged the Will, is allowed to remain inactive and not employed.

The strong men and women of the world invariably manifest the Masculine Principle of Will, and their strength depends materially upon this fact. Instead of living upon the impressions made upon their minds by others, they dominate their own minds by their Will, obtaining the kind of mental images desired, and moreover dominate the minds of others likewise, in the same manner. Look at the strong people, how they manage to implant their seed-thoughts in the minds of the masses of the people, thus causing the latter to think thoughts in accordance with the desires and wills of the strong individuals. This is why the masses of people are such sheep-like creatures, never originating an idea of their own, nor using their own powers of mental activity.

The manifestation of Mental Gender may be noticed all around us in everyday life. The magnetic persons are those who are able to use the Masculine Principle in the way of impressing their ideas upon others. The actor who makes people weep or cry as he wills, is employing this principle. and so is the successful orator, statesman, preacher, writer or other people who are before the public attention. The peculiar influence exerted by some people over others is due to the manifestation of Mental Gender, along the Vibrational lines above indicated. In this principle lies the secret of personal magnetism, personal influence, fascination, etc., as well as the phenomena

generally grouped under the name of Hypnotism.

The student who has familiarized himself with the phenomena generally spoken of as "psychic" will have discovered the important part played in the said phenomena by that force which science has styled "Suggestion," by which term is meant the process or method whereby an idea is transferred to, or "impressed upon" the mind of another, causing the second mind to act in accordance therewith. A correct understanding of Suggestion is necessary in order to intelligently comprehend the varied psychical phenomena which Suggestion underlies. But, still more is a knowledge of Vibration and Mental Gender necessary for the student of Suggestion. For the whole principle of Suggestion depends upon the principle of Mental Gender and Vibration.

It is customary for the writers and teachers of Suggestion to explain that it is the "objective or voluntary" mind which make the mental impression, or suggestion, upon the "subjective or involuntary" mind. But they do not describe the process or give us any analogy in nature whereby we may more readily comprehend the idea. But if you will think of the matter in the light of the Hermetic Teachings you will be able to see that the energizing of the Feminine Principle by the Vibratory Energy of the Masculine Principle Is in accordance to the universal laws of nature, and that the natural world affords countless analogies whereby the principle may be understood. In fact, the Hermetic Teachings show that the very creation of the Universe follows the same law, and that in all creative manifestations, upon the planes of the spiritual, the mental, and the physical, there is always in operation this principle of Gender—this manifestation of the Masculine and the Feminine Principles. "As above, so below; as below, so above." And more than this, when the principle of Mental Gender is once grasped and understood, the varied phenomena of psychology at once becomes capable of intelligent classification and study, instead of being very much in the dark. The principle "works out" in practice, because it is based upon the immutable universal laws of life.

We shall not enter into an extended discussion of, or description of, the varied phenomena of mental influence or psychic activity. There are many books, many of them quite good, which have been written and published on this subject of late years. The main facts stated in these various books are correct, although the several writers have attempted to explain the phenomena by various pet theories of their own. The student may acquaint himself with these matters, and by using the theory of Mental Gender he will be able to bring order out of the chaos of conflicting theory and teachings, and may, moreover, readily make himself a master of the subject if he be so inclined. The purpose of this work is not to give an extended account of psychic phenomena but rather to give to the student a master-key whereby He

may unlock the many doors leading into the parts of the Temple of Knowledge which he may wish to explore. We feel that in this consideration of the teachings of The Kybalion, one may find an explanation which will serve to clear away many perplexing difficulties—a key that will unlock many doors. What is the use of going into detail regarding all of the many features of psychic phenomena and mental science, provided we place in the hands of the student the means whereby he may acquaint himself fully regarding any phase of the subject which may interest him. With the aid of The Kybalion one may go through any occult library anew, the old Light from Egypt illuminating many dark pages, and obscure subjects. That is the purpose of this book. We do not come expounding a new philosophy, but rather furnishing the outlines of a great world-old teaching which will make clear the teachings of others—which will serve as a Great Reconciler of differing: theories, and opposing doctrines.

Chapter XV. Hermetic Axioms

"The possession of Knowledge, unless accompanied by a manifestation and expression in Action, is like the hoarding of precious metals—a vain and foolish thing. Knowledge, like wealth, is intended for Use. The Law of Use is Universal, and he who violates it suffers by reason of his conflict with natural forces."—*The Kybalion.*

The Hermetic Teachings, while always having been kept securely locked up in the minds of the fortunate possessors thereof, for reasons which we have already stated, were never intended to be merely stored away and secreted. The Law of Use is dwelt upon in the Teachings, as you may see by reference to the above quotation from The Kybalion, which states it forcibly. Knowledge without Use and Expression is a vain thing, bringing no good to its possessor, or to the race. Beware of Mental Miserliness, and express into Action that which you have learned. Study the Axioms and Aphorisms, but practice them also.

We give below some of the more important Hermetic Axioms, from The Kybalion, with a few comments added to each. Make these your own, and practice and use them, for they are not really your own until you have Used them.

"To change your mood or mental state—change your vibration."— *The Kybalion.*

One may change his mental vibrations by an effort of Will, in the direction of deliberately fixing the Attention upon a more desirable state. Will directs the Attention, and Attention changes the Vibration. Cultivate the Art of Attention, by means of the Will, and you have solved the secret of the Mastery of Moods and Mental States.

"To destroy an undesirable rate of mental vibration, put into operation the principle of Polarity and concentrate upon the opposite pole to that which you desire to suppress. Kill out the undesirable by changing its polarity."—*The Kybalion.*

This is one of the most important of the Hermetic Formulas. It is based upon true scientific principles. We have shown you that a mental state and its opposite were merely the two poles of one thing, and that by Mental Transmutation the polarity might be reversed. This Principle is known to modern psychologists, who apply it to the breaking up of undesirable habits by bidding their students concentrate upon the opposite quality. If you are possessed of Fear, do not waste time trying to "kill out" Fear, but instead cultivate the quality of Courage, and the Fear will disappear. Some writers have expressed this idea most forcibly by using the illustration of the dark room. You do not have to shovel out or sweep out the Darkness, but by merely opening the shutters and letting in the Light the Darkness has disappeared. To kill

out a Negative quality, concentrate upon the Positive Pole of that same quality, and the vibrations will gradually change from Negative to Positive, until finally you will become polarized on the Positive pole instead of the Negative. The reverse is also true, as many have found out to their sorrow, when they have allowed themselves to vibrate too constantly on the Negative pole of things. By changing your polarity you may master your moods, change your mental states, remake your disposition, and build up character. Much of the Mental Mastery of the advanced Hermetics is due to this application of Polarity, which is one of the important aspects of Mental Transmutation. Remember the Hermetic Axiom (quoted previously), which says:

"Mind (as well as metals and elements) may be transmuted from state to state degree to degree. condition to condition pole to pole; vibration to vibration."—*The Kybalion.*

The mastery of Polarization is the mastery of the fundamental principles of Mental Transmutation or Mental Alchemy, for unless one acquires the art of changing his own polarity, he will be unable to affect his environment. An understanding of this principle will enable one to change his own Polarity, as well as that of others, if he will but devote the time, care, study and practice necessary to master the art. The principle is true, but the results obtained depend upon the persistent patience and practice of the student.

"Rhythm may be neutralized by an application of the Art of Polarization."—*The Kybalion.*

As we have explained in previous chapters, the Hermetists hold that the Principle of Rhythm manifests on the Mental Plane as well as on the Physical Plane, and that the bewildering succession of moods, feelings, emotions, and other mental states, are due to the backward and forward swing of the mental pendulum, which carries us from one extreme of feeling to the other. The Hermetists also teach that the Law of Neutralization enables one, to a great extent, to overcome the operation of Rhythm in consciousness. As we have explained, there is a Higher Plane of Consciousness, as well as the ordinary Lower Plane, and the Master by rising mentally to the Higher Plane causes the swing of the mental pendulum to manifest on the Lower Plane, and he, dwelling on his Higher Plane, escapes the consciousness of the swing backward. This is effected by polarizing on the Higher Self, and thus raising the mental vibrations of the Ego above those of the ordinary plane of consciousness. It is akin to rising above a thing and allowing it to pass beneath you. The advanced Hermetist polarizes himself at the Positive Pole of his Being—the "I Am" pole rather than the pole of personality and by "refusing" and "denying" the operation of Rhythm, raises himself above its plane of consciousness, and standing firm in his Statement of Being he allows the pendulum to swing back on the Lower Plane without changing his Polarity. This is accomplished by all

individuals who have attained any degree of self-mastery, whether they understand the law or not. Such persons simply "refuse" to allow themselves to be swung back by the pendulum of mood and emotion, and by steadfastly affirming the superiority they remain polarized on the Positive pole. The Master, of course, attains a far greater degree of proficiency, because he understands the law which he is overcoming by a higher law, and by the use of his Will he attains a degree of Poise and Mental Steadfastness almost impossible of belief on the part of those who allow themselves to be swung backward and forward by the mental pendulum of moods and feelings.

Remember always, however, that you do not really destroy the Principle of Rhythm, for that is indestructible. You simply overcome one law by counter-balancing it with another and thus maintain an equilibrium. The laws of balance and counter-balance are in operation on the mental as well as on the physical planes, and an understanding of these laws enables one to seem to overthrow laws, whereas he is merely exerting a counterbalance.

"Nothing escapes the Principle of Cause and Effect, but there are many Planes of Causation, and one may use the laws of the higher to overcome the laws of the lower."—*The Kybalion.*

By an understanding of the practice of Polarization, the Hermetists rise to a higher plane of Causation and thus counter-balance the laws of the lower planes of Causation. By rising above the plane of ordinary Causes they become themselves, in a degree, Causes instead of being merely Caused. By being able to master their own moods and feelings, and by being able to neutralize Rhythm, as we have already explained, they are able to escape a great part of the operations of Cause and Effect on the ordinary plane. The masses of people are carried along, obedient to their environment; the wills and desires of others stronger than themselves; the effects of inherited tendencies; the suggestions of those about them; and other outward causes; which tend to move them about on the chess-board of life like mere pawns. By rising above these influencing causes, the advanced Hermetists seek a higher plane of mental action, and by dominating their moods, emotions, impulses and feelings, they create for themselves new characters, qualities and powers, by which they overcome their ordinary environment, and thus become practically players instead of mere Pawns. Such people help to play the game of life understandingly, instead of being moved about this way and that way by stronger influences and powers and wills. They use the Principle of Cause and Effect, instead of being used by it. Of course, even the highest are subject to the Principle as it manifests on the higher planes, but on the lower planes of activity, they are Masters instead of Slaves. As The Kybalion says:

"The wise ones serve on the higher, but rule on the lower. They obey the laws coming from above them, But on their own plane, and

those below them they rule and give orders. And, yet, in so doing, they form a part of the Principle, instead of opposing it. The wise man falls in with the Law, and by understanding its movements he operates it instead of being its blind slave. Just as does the skilled swimmer turn this way and that way, going and coming as he will, instead of being as the log which is carried here and there—so is the wise man as compared to the ordinary man—and yet both swimmer and log; wise man and fool, are subject to Law. He who understands this is well on the road to Mastery."—*The Kybalion.*

In conclusion let us again call your attention to the Hermetic Axiom:

"True Hermetic Transmutation is a Mental Art."—*The Kybalion.*

In the above axiom, the Hermetists teach that the great work of influencing one's environment is accomplished by Mental Power. The Universe being wholly mental, it follows that it may be ruled only by Mentality. And in this truth is to be found an explanation of all the phenomena and manifestations of the various mental powers which are attracting so much attention and study in these earlier years of the Twentieth Century. Back of and under the teachings of the various cults and schools, remains ever constant the Principle of the Mental Substance of the Universe. If the Universe be Mental in its substantial nature, then it follows that Mental Transmutation must change the conditions and phenomena of the Universe. If the Universe is Mental, then Mind must be the highest power affecting its phenomena. If this be understood then all the so-called "miracles" and "wonder-workings" are seen plainly for what they are.

"THE ALL is MIND; The Universe is Mental."—*The Kybalion.*

THE END